THE SPIRIT OF SIMPLE LIVING

Simple Retirement

SHARON HANBY-ROBIE

Guideposts.
CARMEL, NEW YORK 10512

Acknowledgments

Every attempt has been made to credit the sources of copyrighted material used in this book. If any such acknowledgment has been inadvertently omitted or miscredited, receipt of such information would be appreciated.

All material that originally appeared in *Daily Guideposts* is reprinted with permission.

www.guideposts.org
1-800-431-2344
Guideposts Books & Inspirational Media Division
Developmental Editors: Cristine Bolley and Deb Strubel
Cover design by Diane Bonder
Interior design by Cindy LaBreacht
Photo by Philip Coblentz/Digital Vision/Getty Images
Typeset by Nancy Tardi
Printed in the United States of America

Contents

Introduction

Retirement is something that many of us have dreamt about. Yet, nowhere in the Bible could I find anyone who "retired." In fact, Moses lived to the age of one hundred twenty and accomplished his greatest feats in his later years. Experts say that we should consider ourselves fortunate; we are living longer and enjoying better health than many recent generations. Technology is increasing rapidly, and we have exciting options through which to enjoy our lives that are unprecedented in *any* previous generation. In addition, we have an overall level of financial independence unmatched in history.

Those facts suggest that God may have a divine purpose for keeping us on earth longer than our forefathers. Perhaps, instead of simply retiring we are meant to take all the years of experience and knowledge that we have and apply our natural and spiritual gifts to God's work.

Thoughts of retirement force us to face a lot of truths about ourselves. In fact, our number one priority in planning for retirement probably should start with our getting to really know ourselves and the values that guide us, so that we are prepared to make sound retirement decisions based on those principles.

Our individual personalities, health and financial resources will certainly affect how we define retirement. Some of us may never retire, but instead use this time as an opportunity to change careers and focus on more rewarding work. The more energetic among us may even use this time to start new businesses of their own. And others may find themselves responsible for family members who need physical and financial support. Some may experience retirement as the loneliest time of their lives.

Having a strong and well-developed faith is important for all of life, but for our later years it is critical. These years should be the best part of our spiritual journey. And part of that journey should be to think about what kind of footprint we will leave when we move on to eternity. None of us knows the future. None of us knows when we will die or the exact circumstances, financial or otherwise, that we may encounter along the way. As you read through this book, I will travel with you and try to impart some guidance to help make your journey one of spiritual blessings—and joy.

—Sharon Hanby-Robie

PART ONE

Passionate about Retirement

GOD HAS ORDAINED SEASONS IN OUR LIVES for new experiences, and our retirement years offer the best years of our lives. Using our spiritual gifts, natural talents and life resources to serve the Lord in our latter years is perhaps life's greatest opportunity to feel fulfilled. In retirement, we will have more time for interpersonal relationships than ever before. This is a time for spouses to enjoy closer friendships with each other and for us to develop new friendships with people outside of our existing contacts. Everyone shares the common goal of retirement, but not everyone seizes this great opportunity to explore new lifestyle options and finally achieve lifelong goals. After reading these first few pages, you will know that your best years are still ahead.

Defining Retirement

> **Moses was a hundred and twenty years old when he died, yet his eyes were not weak nor his strength gone.**
>
> —DEUTERONOMY 34:7 (NIV)

Moses' great accomplishments were reserved for the last forty years of his life. The man who had dreamed of helping his people was given that very mission by God. Armed with a new revelation of God's name and with the divine promises, Moses set out on a journey back to Egypt, where God's people were enslaved. Moses led the new generation of Israelites along the east bank of the Jordan, defeating the people who lived there. Camped across the Jordan from Jericho, Moses reviewed the Law and cast it in the form of a treaty between a ruler and his people, which we now know as the book of Deuteronomy. Moses faithfully kept on course despite discouragement and occasional despair. He was a man who performed great deeds with the strength that only God can provide.

Moses was amazing, and he never stopped working for God; he did not retire. In fact, nowhere in the Bible have I found anyone who "retired." Our current retirement age of sixty-five was chosen by Chancellor Otto Von Bismark of

Germany in the 1880s, when only 1.5 percent of the population even lived past that age. While today's target retirement age is still sixty-five, a person can actually live thirty years longer than that. I don't think this extension of life is pure coincidence. Researchers say that better health practices, quality food, control of disease and modern medicine all contribute to longevity. And longevity might just be God's plan for our generation.

According to certified retirement success coach Diane D'Agostino, we baby boomers, the current generation of up and coming retirees, truly have been blessed. We have been given the equivalent of thirty extra years of life. We are part of the most highly educated and skilled generation in history. We have a level of financial independence unmatched at any time in history. And, generally speaking, we are in better shape physically and mentally than previous generations. We are more adaptable and more ready to take on new challenges than any generation in past history. That prompted D'Agostino to wonder: "Has it occurred to you that these blessings might not simply be human progress, but instead come from the hand of God and that God must have blessed you with them with a specific purpose in mind? Those extra years, education, skill and financial independence may not just be your reward for years of hard work but rather are intended for your use in your new career serving God and humanity?"

I don't know about you, but when I thought about the answer to that question, it gave me goose bumps. God has placed each one of us in a specific time and place for His purpose. Of course, He also plans the years we will live and when we will die so that we can accomplish that purpose. Without purpose, we are miserably discontent. Without challenges and new visions, we become depressed.

Nancy Schlossberg, EdD, author of *Retire Smart, Retire Happy: Finding*

Your True Path in Life, says, "Articles and books on retirement pay much attention to ways to replace financial capital, but few focus on ways to replace psychological or social capital." One woman she counseled said she felt guilty because she was living the "American Dream," but had not found life meaningful.[1] She had been unable to create a retirement life that was satisfying.

One retired professor summed up his retirement woes this way: "Suddenly you are on your own." While he was working, the staff had always come in early to have coffee and chat. He missed the easy camaraderie. Another woman, who chose to retire when her husband did, found herself unable to define the problem—she simply felt empty. Worse yet, she was angry with herself for not being able to adapt. Schlossberg helped her realize that she had neither acknowledged nor mourned her loss of camaraderie. She didn't miss the work; she missed her workplace and the social environment of support that it had given her.

Unfortunately, most of us spend forty years building a financial nest egg, but no time thinking about how we are going to enjoy retirement. Schlossberg says that work furnishes a sense of place and a membership in a valued community. "This sense of place and belonging in turn provides individuals with feelings of worth."

HOW DO YOU WANT TO SPEND THE REST OF YOUR LIFE?

Figuring out what we really want in retirement is critical to finding it rewarding. Advocates of life planning say we should find a holistic approach that considers our most deeply held values instead of focusing exclusively on how much money we can accumulate for retirement. George Kinder, founder of a small group of planners who advocate this approach, suggests that his clients imagine that they have enough money to take care of all their needs, both now and in the future. Then he throws out three questions: How would you live your life? What would you do with the money? Would you change anything? He urges clients not to hold back. He wants them to visualize the life of their dreams in the greatest possible detail.

Once Kinder has taken his clients through this imagery, he takes them a step further, suggesting they imagine that their doctors just told them that they have five to ten years left to live. He tells them they will be healthy up until they die, but they won't know exactly when they will die. Then he asks them three additional questions: What will you do in the time you have remaining to live? Will it change your life? If so, how will you change it?

And just to make things really interesting, he takes them even further in confronting their mortality when he tells his clients that they are to imagine that they have just *one* day left to live. He asks them to pay close attention to the emotions that arise as they face these last questions: What dreams will be left unfulfilled? What do I wish I had finished or had been? What do I wish I had done? What did I miss?

It is only by going through this scenario and list of questions that we can identify core values that can be incorporated into our day-to-day living. The path to a happy retirement is finding meaning and purpose for it. Guideposts writer Marion Bond West was fortunate enough to meet an amazing woman who had discovered the secret to such a meaningful life:

> The first time I ever heard Miss Bertha Smith speak, she was past eighty-five. *Goodness*, I thought, *this dear little woman will never get through the seminar—four hours daily for five days, standing!* I realized during the first minutes of her

dynamic message how wrong I had been to judge her by age. This gentle-looking woman spoke with authority and power. She seemed never to tire. I've heard young ministers tell with amazement how none of them could keep up with "Miss Bertha." No one I know has ever seen Miss Bertha tired. Oh, she retired as a foreign missionary at the proper age, but she did not retire from the Lord's Army. She continues her ministry of loving and sharing God's message in her unique, uncompromising style.

She says that her remarkable secret is that she does nothing in her own strength and keeps her sins confessed up. "It's all Him," she says matter-of-factly, believing that age is no excuse whatsoever for being inactive.

Miss Bertha lives in Cowpens, South Carolina, but travels extensively. She's an amazing woman. But perhaps most amazing of all is that at ninety-eight she is booked solid until she is one hundred and five to speak for the Lord. (Miss Bertha died at age one hundred in 1988.)

SIMPLICITY MADE SIMPLE

ASK YOURSELF THE TOUGH QUESTIONS before you collect your gold watch. Consider the questions posed by Schlossberg and then tackle a few more. Glenn Ruffenach wrote an article for *The Wall Street Journal Sunday* in which he presented four questions for getting your retirement life on track: "Can the next step in my life be truly revitalizing?" Retirement can be an opportunity to begin anew and transform your life and reinvent yourself. "How will I structure my time?" For some people, free time produces anxiety. In an attempt to fill their days they actually take on too many responsibilities (volunteer work, school, a part-time job). Then they realize that this is not what they want to do. Ruffenach says, "The point is to be more discriminating. Sure, you can fill your time—that's easy. You have to ask yourself: What do I really care about?

RETIRE ONE STEP AT A TIME. Phased retirement is a new idea that seems to be working well both for employers and employees. It may be the best way to ease into a new lifestyle. Some workers are choosing to work a four-day week, compressing forty hours into four ten-hour days. One gentleman who worked for The Hartford Financial Services Group said, "It gave me a chance to begin seeing what extra time at home would be like. It also got my wife used to having me around, and knowing that I was coming into her territory." A growing number of people are eager to keep one foot planted firmly in the workplace, while they enjoy more leisure time and cultivate new activities. Phased retirement gives older employees more flexibility with less responsibility. If this is something you would like to consider, be sure to talk finances with your employer. Most companies calculate retirement benefits on pay earned during the last few years of work. Those who cut their hours and salaries early may reduce future pensions. To avoid that problem, some companies, including The Hartford, calculate pension benefits on the basis of the highest five years of salary during the past ten years of employment.

Create your own "phased" retirement. Five years prior to retiring, **TAKE STEPS TO EASE THE TRANSITION**. Jeri Sedlar, cofounder of Sedlar & Miners, a New York City-based executive search and transition coaching firm, says,

"Mentor young executives so that they have a reason to come to you with future problems . . . look into becoming a consultant . . . join organizations or associations with an eye toward future leadership positions."

CHOOSE TO DO WHAT MAKES YOU HAPPY. Perhaps the best part of reaching retirement age is having the opportunity to finally do what you may always have wanted to do. Jean Cherni of Branford, Connecticut, started her own business, Senior Living Solutions, serving as a retirement adviser and moving consultant three years after she retired from a twenty-five-year career as a real estate broker. She says, "Finally, at seventy-five, I'm doing what I want to do." She illustrates a pattern of later-life employment that is becoming more common as older workers create jobs that are part-time, flexible and entrepreneurial. A study shows that among those in their early to midsixties who are still employed, forty-four percent work in arrangements other than regular full-time jobs. The key is finding meaningful work that allows us to have quality of life while spending more time with elderly parents, grandchildren and friends.

Lord, forgive me for losing sight of the exciting future You have in store for me. Instead of regretting the loss of good times, I will listen for Your voice to lead me to new opportunities to serve You and expect my latter years to be greater than my former ones. Amen.

What's Your Personality?

Retiring is just practicing up to be dead.
That doesn't take any practice.

—PAUL HARVEY, AMERICAN RADIO BROADCASTER

My mother tells me I would be bored to tears if I wasn't busy. She's probably right. I'm a lot like Mom in this way. She is seventy-two and still happily working four days a week. She too would be bored if she quit working. She has a lot of good friends and plenty of family to keep her social life full. She has a great outlook on life and loves what she does. Fortunately, she is also blessed with good health. Mom and I do not have the kind of personality that would be content with simply taking it easy.

My father, on the other hand, couldn't wait to retire. His job required a lot of physical labor, which certainly affected his desire to retire. But Dad had a different attitude about life in general. He often saw the glass of life as half empty rather than half full. My sister can't wait to retire. She loves gardening and wants to have more time to spend in her garden and putter around her house. She doesn't understand Mom or me—she thinks we're crazy to want to keep so busy.

Our personalities will have a lot to do with how we will structure and manage our time in retirement. Some people will find it difficult to manage life without the structure of an organized schedule. Others will thrive on the flexibility that retirement offers. Nancy Schlossberg, mentioned earlier, has found that there are basically five different retirement personality types. Each one will approach and manage retirement in a characteristic way.

Perhaps you are an *Easy Glider*. Easy Gliders are retirees who "enjoy unscheduled time, select activities that appeal to them and pace themselves according to their newfound freedom. They want to relax and embrace the retirement ride—sometimes meandering, sometimes working and sometimes simply being involved with family and friends." My sister is probably an Easy Glider.

Or are you a *Continuer*? Schlossberg says, "Continuers package their principal activities in new ways. They do this by staying connected with their past skills, activities, interests and values, but they modify them to fit retirement." A good example of this would be someone who chose to become a consultant for the industry he or she used to work within. Being self-employed would offer more control, which would allow room to balance a work schedule with other activities. My mother is a lot like this. She went from managing a kitchen-remodeling business to working for a company as a kitchen and bath designer.

"*Adventurers* see retirement as an opportunity to start new endeavors. They love to find new ways of organizing their personal time and space." Adventurers are willing to invest in developing new skills that reenergize them. I'm a lot like that. I love taking on new projects that give me the chance to learn new skills while incorporating my current level of expertise.

A lot of us will fall into the *Searcher* personality category—at least temporarily. Schlossberg writes, "Because retirement is a time of exploring new options for life structure and activities, it is a path marked by trial and error. It is not unusual for a retiree to start on one path, find that it is not satisfying, and to resume searching."

The last personality type that Schlossberg identified in her book is the *Retreater*. She says that sometimes it can be difficult to tell whether Retreaters are just taking time out—a short-term moratorium from life—or whether they are disengaging from life entirely.

IT'S FINALLY TIME TO LIVE YOUR DREAM

Identifying your personality (or combination of personality characteristics) can help you figure out what path your retirement life will take. In fact, your number one priority in planning for retirement should be to really get to know yourself, your values and the principles that guide your life, so that you will be prepared to make good decisions for retirement that are based on those values.

By the time we reach midlife, most of us have gone through a stage where being part of a group has been paramount to our lives. We have had to learn to minimize our own personality and desires, at least on a subconscious level, to conform to the norm. This can be especially true in the workplace, but it is also true for families. Certainly, having children puts you in this position—naturally, they come first. As they grow and leave the nest, things change.

Jim McMichael, an adjunct professor who teaches on aging and who counsels people on retirement at Florida State University, says, "This is the time when we begin to individuate; to get to know ourselves and to begin to make lifetime decisions based on that knowledge. In my years of working with older people and retirement counseling, the happiest people I have met and worked with are people that have gone through that process, [who] can look back at their life with a good deal of satisfaction. Those that were most miserable were those who when they looked back at their lives realized that they continually sublimated themselves and their personalities to espouse a family, a social group, a community, a church or what-have-you." McMichael agrees that these things should be taken into consideration and are important. But what is also important is that we make conscious decisions regarding all those relationships based on a thorough knowledge and understanding of ourselves and our values too.

Ernie Zelinski, author of *How to Retire Happy, Wild, and Free*, says, "For most of us, a happy retirement won't be attained by freedom from duty and responsibility, leading to a life filled with nothing but passive leisure and pleasure . . . The vast majority of North American workers spend their leisure time watching a lot of TV, or doing other activities that provide little personal satisfaction. . . . These activities, however, are poor preparation for a retirement that is happy, wild, and free. Only by being physically, intellectually, and creatively challenged can individuals find satisfaction and fulfillment in their leisure activities."

To summarize, in order to retire we must prepare financially, but we must also get to really know ourselves, find interesting hobbies, explore new activities, discover God's purpose for this stage of life and develop all the necessary skills to accomplish it. It's beginning to sound like a lot of work to simply retire! Perhaps, we'd better keep working—just kidding. I know that the process of preparing for a change in our future lifestyle will lead us to greater self-awareness and give us greater insight into uncovering new opportunities. The process of preparing for something new will also, most importantly, give us insight into the nature of our Creator in whose image we have been designed.

SIMPLICITY MADE SIMPLE

BE HAPPY, STAY HEALTHY. McMichael says there is a relationship between being reasonably happy with yourself and your chances for being healthy. He says, "Unhappy people tend to be unhealthy people. And I happen to believe it is the unhappiness that drives the unhealthiness. However, none of us can take our health for granted." Find interests that perk you up. This may be crucial if you now have an empty nest after spending the past twenty years being a stay-at-home mom, dedicated solely to caring for your family without the opportunity to invest in yourself. A study by psychologist Joseph Kuypers in the 1970s found that "if a woman's only interest in her thirties had been her husband and children, she was more likely to be unhappy in later life. Some people who had chafed at being just wives and mothers were more fulfilled in their seventies because for the first time they found what fit them. They had never liked the housewife role. At seventy they were finally able to live as they wanted—to have a career."

ARRANGE YOUR OUTER LIFE TO FIT YOUR INNER PERSON. A study published in 1987 found that it was crucial to arrange an outer life that fits us. Jane Belsky reported in her book, *Here Tomorrow: Making the Most of Life after Fifty*, that Rutgers University psychologist Daniel Ogilvie asked a group of retirement-aged men and women to rank their "identities," the life roles that were most meaningful to them (e.g., mother, gardener, choir member, caregiver to ailing mother, highly organized person, pillar of the community). He then asked how much time they actually spent acting out these most meaningful aspects of themselves and probed their morale. People who spent the most time living out their highest-ranking identities were also the happiest people.

Analyze your life. Belsky says we should systematically analyze our lives: "After reframing your attitudes, **YOU NEED TO DECIDE WHAT SPECIFIC DIRECTIONS TO PURSUE**." She recommends that we list our most meaningful roles, our prized traits and skills, and the aspect of ourselves that we value most (e.g., musician, good cook, giving person, organizer). She recommends that you "assess how much time you actually spend enacting these most meaningful duties. Then devise specific strategies to increase this time."[2] She says, for example, some might find that volunteering to help homeless people find shelter and negotiate the system might be tailor-made to satisfying their need to give to others and draw on existing talents as an organizer. Belsky also says that if your list of perceived skills is meager, then it is an indication that you need to construct some new and compelling roles for yourself. She recommends evaluating your life. Are there interests, activities or new roles that you haven't attempted but you think you might enjoy? If so, what's stopping you?

Explore your past. **TAKE THE TIME TO REMEMBER WHAT USED TO INTEREST YOU.** Belsky says, "When we begin by going through the motions of doing something that used to thrill us but that we can't imagine enjoying now, an emotional connection is sometimes remade. Almost magically, the good feeling starts flowing again."[3]

Lord, stir in me the goals I have laid aside that were truly inspired by You. Direct me on the path of usefulness and complete in me the destiny of Your design that I have yet to fulfill. Amen.

Together 24/7!

Love is very patient and kind. . . . Love does not demand its own way. It is not irritable or touchy. . . .

—1 CORINTHIANS 13:4, 5 (TLB)

Perhaps you can relate to this story by Guideposts writer Fay Angus, especially if you have been a stay-at-home wife.

> Sure enough, he was right on cue! I watched from the kitchen window as, with some effort, he uncurled his lanky frame from the flowerbeds where he had spent the last hour pulling weeds. He checked his watch. *Any time now*, I could almost hear him think, as only wives can hear their husbands think.
>
> He unlatched the garden gate and walked briskly to the mailbox, its bright red flag waiting to be lowered. Resentment bubbled up within me. For the twenty-seven years of our married life, each

afternoon *I* had gotten the mail. It was the highlight of my day. A three o'clock cup of tea, then sorting, sifting and stacking—bills underneath, periodicals and catalogs on the side, the open-me-first priority of personal letters right on top. But since his retirement, daily *he* had been getting the mail. With irritation I watched him stand thumbing through it, then lay it on a rock until he had finished putting his tools away, unaware of my cooling cup of tea and impatient waiting.

"He's invading my space, unsettling my schedule!" I complained to a friend.

She smiled. "Have you thought that for all those years *you* have had the pleasure of the mail—and maybe now *he*'s entitled?"

Her reply brought me and my complaint into focus. This most honorable man, who had spent over half a lifetime working hard to provide a comfortable living for the children and me—this dedicated man, who served his Lord with joy and gladness—indeed, he was entitled!

My love gift to him: *John-who-gets-the-mail, you are entitled!*

The mere thought of your retired husband suddenly being with you 24/7 and expecting you to give up your own independence to fill his days can strain even the best of relationships. My friend's husband insisted that she retire when he did, despite the fact that she is ten years younger than him. Why? Because he wanted her to play golf with him—in other words, he needed a playmate! But she loved her job and was thoroughly enjoying it. He also loved sailing; she tolerated it. She loved gardening, and he tolerated it. None of those things were big issues while he was working. But now . . . trouble was brewing. And they are not alone in this.

In fact, it is not unusual for couples over the age of sixty to divorce even after being married for decades. According to psychologist Sara Yogev, "Retirees now face one-quarter of their lifetimes without the jobs that bolstered their self-esteem—and helped them overlook the problems in their relationships." Retirement is the surprising marriage wrecker for many couples. "In other words, the relationship after retirement changes from two people being together but independent to two people sharing one life together," according to the authors of *The Healing Journey Through Retirement: Your Journal of Transition and Transformation.*

EXPECT AND EMBRACE CHANGE

The reality is that most marriages do change after retirement—but it doesn't have to be for the worse. However, as the authors of *The Healing Journey Through Retirement* noted, "When major marital conflict does occur *during* retirement, it's likely to be a continuation of long-standing problems that were ignored or unresolved *before* retirement."[4] They believe that the keys to a successful postretirement marriage are honesty, empathy and an effort to anticipate the changes in the rhythms of your own routine and those of your partner. It is critical to resolve big issues that could affect both partners. But it is also important to resolve the "small stuff," daily annoyances such as who collects the mail, as Fay Angus finally learned with a little help from her friend.

Jane Belsky believes that there are basically three different types of marriages. The "conflicted" marriage uses quarreling and nagging as its form of communication. These couples seem locked in a never-ending war—but they don't seem interested in divorce. It is as if they derive some kind of weird pleasure from having someone with whom to fight. The "passive/congenial" marriage is less stormy but no more fulfilling. Couples stay together but are emotionally separated. They seem to have nothing in common—"no real love or closeness." The third kind of marriage that Belsky defines is "the vital relationship." Belsky observes that vital pairs can be easily overlooked. "They do the same things, publicly at least, and when talking they say the same things—they are proud of their homes, love their children, gripe about their jobs. . . . But when we take a close, intimate look, the vital quality of the relationship becomes clear; the mates are intensely bound together psychologically in important life matters. The relationship provides the life essence for both man and woman."[5]

There is good news and bad news in terms of being one of the lucky vital couples. Love can deepen over the years, but rarely does something grow from nothing. If you have never really loved your spouse or had a satisfactory relationship prior to retirement, then it will be really, really tough to make it so after retirement. For other couples though, the second half of marriage can be the better half if they are willing to accept change. As we all know, change is hard—even when it is for our own good.

Mike Yorkey, author of *Your Fabulous Fifties*, says couples he interviewed admitted that they needed to be reminded that life is a series of adjustments, that changes are as certain as the seasons. "As you face the second half of your marriage, embrace change—but embrace it together." The greatest indicator of a long-term successful marriage is the friendship of the couple. "In other words, you need to become best friends!" says Yorkey.[6]

Prepare for the mental and emotional changes that may come. Stephen Treat, director and CEO of the Council for Relationships, says, "It's important to sit down face-to-face, with no TV, no newspaper. **COUPLES SHOULD TALK ABOUT RETIREMENT AND START TO ANTICIPATE IT**, along with ideas about what roles (masculine and feminine) they're now going to play. They should talk about how much time they want to spend together." He says that although it's hard to talk about not spending all your time together without hurting the other person's feelings, it's a conversation you need to have. He suggests asking the difficult questions in a loving way, like: "How are we going to be as individuals and how are we going to be as a couple?" He says these conversations should be started at least five years before you intend to retire.

AIR YOUR EXPECTATIONS. For many couples, the wife has managed their social calendar throughout the marriage. Many retiring husbands simply assume that their wives will keep them busy in retirement too. The reality is that millions of women continue to work after their husbands retire. Even if a woman does stop working, she shouldn't be expected to plan her husband's day. Jeri Sedlar, cofounder of Sedlar and Miners, a New York City-based transition coaching firm, interviewed one woman who had this to say about her husband's inevitable retirement, "I don't want twice the husband for half the pay." I think that is very well put. Besides, is there anything wrong with expecting your husband to have his own friends and activities? Sedlar recommends that we all develop activities separate from our spouses *before* we retire.

BE OPEN TO NEW DIVISIONS OF LABOR. This is another recommendation from Yogev: "It's smart for spouses to share tasks. Besides making the relationship more equal, learning such skills is essential if a mate becomes sick or dies." She suggests identifying the chores each likes and hates. For example, if your husband hates cooking and laundry—then let him do the grocery shopping and washing the dishes after meals.

Organize your time. Schedule "couples" activities and social events. Yogev says, "This formalizes being a couple again and gives you the sense of structure you had before retirement." But **BE SURE TO SCHEDULE INDIVIDUAL TIME** too. Building social networks and leisure activities prior to retirement can make the later transition much easier.

Find a new purpose. This is especially true for men who have difficulty creating social groups outside a structured setting. Most men suffer an enormous loss of autonomy and self-esteem upon retirement. As a result, many of them turn into grumpy old men. They become oversensitive and irritable. They need to **FIND A NEW PURPOSE, PROJECT OR ACTIVITY** that may provide pleasure and a sense of accomplishment and pride. One dear old friend of mine joined The Salvation Army when he retired. He spent nearly twenty-five years serving with them and was even honored by them a few years before he died. This organization gave him a very fulfilling purpose that made his retirement years worthwhile to many.

Father, help me to see new ways of doing everyday tasks. Nudge me if I become too set in my ways, for I long to enjoy the freshness of each season You create in my life. Amen.

Friends

> Friends are as companions on a journey, who ought to aid each other to persevere in the road to a happier life.
>
> —PYTHAGORAS, GREEK PHILOSOPHER AND MATHEMATICIAN (CIRCA 580 BC–500 BC)

According to one study, we will go through 396 friends in a lifetime but will have only thirty-three at any one time. Of those thirty-three only six at the most will be considered close friends in whom you can confide and trust when you need a shoulder to cry on. According to the study of ten thousand people, "best friends" are not even the ones that you see most often. In fact, it found that most saw their best friends only once in eight weeks. The remainder of the thirty-three were for social support. Some were old co-workers, others old schoolmates or even old neighbors.

I don't know about you, but to me 396 friends seem like a lot of people to have considered as friends, even over a lifetime. And I'm not so sure that I could count six best friends most of the time either. The good news is that according to Laura Carstensen, a Stanford University professor of psychology, we only really need three! She says, "Our data indicates all you really need is three people in your life on whom you can depend. What matters is knowing you're not alone in the world."

The one thing that most experts agree on is that when it comes to retiring well, it is far more important to invest in making friends than saving money. Alicia Tarnowski and psychologist Toni Antonucci, a senior researcher at the University of Michigan Institute for Social Research, conducted a study of 253 people over the age of fifty. "The researchers analyzed how physical health, income, the number of negative life events, including divorce and death of a spouse, experienced in the last four years, and demographic variables, including age and gender, influenced the changes in life satisfaction reported by recent retirees." The most powerful predictor of retirement satisfaction was the size of the person's social network. Those with networks of about sixteen people were more satisfied on average than those who had fewer than ten people in their network.

When I first read this I thought it might be contradicting Carstensen's finding of only needing three people to depend on. However, further reading showed that the Institute for Social Research study only applied to "recent" retirees. Once you get adjusted, you need less emotional support than you did when you first retired. Tarnowski said, "Just having a number of people who provide emotional support, listen to your concerns, and let you know that you're still valued right after you retire seems to make a big difference."

As I wrote in a previous book in this series, *Simple Friendship*, a life-changing event like retirement will significantly affect our friendships. Some friendships will remain; others will change, while some will end. At a time when we most need friends, we may find ourselves facing a social deficit. This will be especially true if you choose to move when you retire, as many do. A lot of people purposely choose to move closer to their grown children, thinking it will provide them with an immediate social network.

Audry Kavka, a psychiatrist at the San Francisco Psychoanalytic Institute, believes that we must figure out where we can establish the richest social network—whether or not that network includes one's children. She says, "It's important for people to start thinking about this early. The question should not be, 'Should I live with my children or not?' but rather, 'What would be most fulfilling to me?'" A study by Swedish researchers found that "the people most likely to benefit from moving may be those whose local ties have deteriorated. Perhaps a spouse has died, or best friends have moved away."

EXPAND YOUR POOL OF FRIENDS

Aristotle said, "Wishing to be friends is quick work, but friendship is a slow ripening fruit." Good friends are forever. Good friends are for keeps. But all of us must face the reality of life that we will, at least temporarily, have to say good-bye to even the best of friends.

One elderly woman named Ellen has been a widow for eleven years. She has kept busy with her friends and family and the years seem to have passed rather quickly. Recently, she has been a bit lonely and quite sad. Over the last eighteen months she's had a number of changes in her life. She has lost four good friends. One friend died. Her other friends have gone for a number of reasons; one remarried and she hardly sees her anymore. Another had a stroke and is in an extended care hospital. Although Ellen visits with her, it's not the same. Her friend Agnes has a lot of family problems right now, and she really doesn't have any time left for her friends. Ellen is grieving the lonely void left in her life from the loss of these precious relationships.

Retirement changes the dynamics of our friendships. Sometimes it's not even your own retirement that makes the difference as Guideposts writer Linda Ching Sledge found out:

> My dear friend Gwen was gone. Room 530, her old office, was empty, the door locked tight. I sat in my office staring at the lunch bag I had brought from home. Every day for years, I had come to the door of that office for advice, gossip and companionship.
>
> My thoughts were broken by the sound of high-heeled shoes tapping down the hall. The footsteps halted outside room 530. Then I heard the jingle of keys and a heavy book bag dropping as the English department's newest teacher arrived.
>
> On my way to the water fountain, I peeked in at the doorway of 530. A woman looked up from the desk as I passed; her face was terribly young and terribly unsure. Had I once looked that way to Gwen? Quickly, I walked on.
>
> It seemed a long way to the water fountain, even longer going back. I saw, as if for the first time, the scuff marks on the walls where students had leaned year after year; the well-worn carpet; bits of tape on the doors where grade sheets had been tacked up every semester, then torn down. When I looked in at the doorway of 530 this time, I saw bare walls and empty bookshelves: a familiar space with a scared young teacher sitting alone.
>
> "Want to go to lunch with an old-timer?" I ventured in my best big-sister fashion. "There's a place down the road that

serves great macaroni and bean soup." *What better way to honor an old friend than by showing a new friend all the tender mercies that have been shown you.*

SIMPLICITY MADE SIMPLE

MAKE NEW FRIENDS. Allen Unrau, who writes a weekly column relating to "real-life" seniors issues in Abbotsford, British Columbia, says, "Seniors who have faced the loss of a good friend in their lives need to put themselves in the "make new friends" mode immediately. Get out and socialize. Volunteer where you can. Invite people over and bake those cinnamon rolls again. Not many folks do that anymore."

CHECK OUT WHAT'S GOING ON IN YOUR COMMUNITY. Programs are popping up around the country to help people learn how to make the transition to retirement. In my mom's hometown of Parma, Ohio, the Oasis Institute holds life-options seminars for lifelong learning. Community colleges are becoming a magnet for learning-how-to-retire efforts as well. Central Florida Community College in Ocala started a program called Pathways to Living, Learning and Serving. The program trains volunteer coaches to work one-on-one with people fifty-five and older. The coaches help participants map out their next steps in life and connect to resources that can assist them.

GET COOKING! Friends who cook together find themselves sharing more than just a meal. Dorothy Cements encouraged five women to gather at her home for an evening. They were going to try to make *café brûlot*. "As soon as we poured on the brandy, the wooden spoon we were stirring with burst into flames," Clements recalls with a laugh. Amid shouts of "stir, stir" and "blow, blow," the flame finally went out. And so was born The Flaming Spoon Dinner Club. "We're a crazy bunch of women," she says of the group of six widows from North Little Rock, Arkansas, who meet once a month for a home-cooked meal and some lighthearted banter. "They're wonderful friends and a great support group." They're also part of a trend. "Across the country, groups of friends, and sometimes strangers, are forming cooking clubs, not just to share a meal but to dish—about food, relationships, and life." The Flaming Spoons are even part of a two-book compilation of recipes by the New York City-based The Cooking Club.

REACH OUT. "Friendship is a two-way street. It is reaching out—not waiting to be accepted before offering friendship," says Jeanette Lockerbie, author of *Fifty Plus*. "It may be even more difficult for the other person, no matter how shy you feel yourself to be." Lockerbie says, "If we go where people are, almost surely 'like attracts like,' and people who have common interests find each other." She also says that feeding friendships does not need to be unduly time-consuming. We can easily contribute to the health of a friendship without neglecting our other responsibilities.[7]

Just as You always have room in Your heart for one more friend, Lord, I, too, will make room for new friends. Please bring people into my life who will want to share in the goodness You have poured into my days. Amen.

Retirement Ricochet—Time to Get a Job

The righteous will flourish like a palm tree. . . .
They will still bear fruit in old age,
they will stay fresh and green.

—PSALM 92:12, 14 (NIV)

This amazing promise in God's Word for the old to bear fruit and flourish represents encouraging prospects for retirees. As we live longer, and are better educated, more skilled and healthier, we can now contribute years, even decades, of significant service to corporations, our communities and our churches. In fact, our "retirement" years may be our best opportunity for employment ever! Since the ranks of the youngest workers and midcareer employees will not be large enough to replace the baby boomers who do decide to quit working, the Bureau of Labor Statistics projects a shortfall of five million workers in the United States by 2010 and fourteen million by 2020. In other words, there may be a severe shortage of skilled and talented workers within a decade or two.

But you don't have to wait that long to "unretire." There are already many previously retired folks who have realized just how valuable numerous corporations and churches think they are. Dick Kiefer retired after working as an appliance salesman for thirty years. He decided it was time to enjoy his hobbies—like fixing up his favorite car. But it wasn't long before Kiefer had a change of heart. "When I retired at sixty-two, I ran out of things to do and the rocking chair wasn't something I was accustomed to." So he set out looking for a job that would blend his interests with his need for health benefits. He landed at Home Depot, which has partnered with AARP to recruit "mature workers." Kiefer said that when Home Depot realized he had thirty years experience—they said, "You're hired! Can you start on Monday?" He started on Monday.

Home Depot is just one company among a growing number that realize the advantages of older workers. Kim Marie Schulze, a Des Moines Home Depot manager, explained the appeal this way: "Great energy, great work ethic and a great opportunity to bring skilled mentors into the store for some of our younger workers who don't have a lot of experience." It's been a great fit for Kiefer too. He said, "I'm a people person. I'm not one to be by myself. Being in retail sales, that's my business. To be with people and do things for people and help people out. I enjoy my work. It's a great life."

What's interesting about unretirement is that it is not associated with poor retirement planning or inadequate retirement resources. Those with employee pensions are no less likely to unretire than others, according to a study by Nicole Maestas for a Rand Corporation labor and population working paper series. She said, "I find no evidence that unretirement is systematically related to preference shocks—that is, finding retirement more worrisome than anticipated." In fact, she found that "nearly one-half of retirees follow a nontraditional path that involves partial retirement and/or a return to the labor force."

GET ON THE ROAD AGAIN

In an article titled "Seasonal Seniors" by Sara Terry, a special correspondent for *The Christian Science Monitor*, I discovered a whole new idea for traveling in a recreational vehicle (RV). Retirees taking to the road in their RVs have created a new American counterculture that has given rise to a new kind of migrant worker: senior citizens who roam the nation's highways and byways, taking on seasonal jobs everywhere from California to Tennessee, and from Alaska to Florida. One couple said, "Our lifestyle has been laid back, nonstressful, and interesting. Sometimes it's challenging, but it's really just a lot of fun."

No one has the exact number of migrating seniors, but some estimates put the number who travel and work in RVs for part or all of the year at around 750,000. These amazing seniors are forging their own alternative lifestyle, complete with the comforts of home. In the process, they are helping to redefine retirement—and what we want from it. They even have their own publication: *Workamper News*, which caters to seniors living the RV life.

What's more amazing though is that increasingly, these older, mobile workers are being sought out by employers across the country who say they value these employees because they bring to their work experience stability, commitment and a strong work ethic. Some of those targeting these seniors are guest ranches, theme parks, traveling fair contractors (time to join the circus!) private campgrounds, public parks and tour operators.

Steve Anderson, the director of human resources at Adventureland theme park, near Des Moines, Iowa, says, "It's the people skills they bring that's so important. And their work ethic, which is definitely from the old school, not from the new." Mr. Anderson caught on early to the seasonal work trend, which some call work camping. In 1990, an older summer employee told him about the *Workamper News* magazine. He began advertising and actively recruiting senior citizens, traveling to RV shows across the country to let people know about job opportunities at Adventureland. Now more than thirty percent of the park's staff is traveling senior citizens. His oldest workers are seventy-nine and eighty-one years of age. Anderson says, "They've become mentors for our young people. Our guests tell us they enjoy seeing older people running the equipment and strapping children into rides. Some of them call it the grandparent approach."

Karen Poppe, who's in charge of hiring at Wall Drugs in Wall, South Dakota, cites the reliability factor. She also claims that seniors know customer service as well as anyone could ever explain it. "We really count on them. They add a lot of stability to what we do."

Churches are benefiting too. Retirees rank high among God's gifts to the church. Retirees are willing to contribute their wisdom, expertise and talents. They have accumulated many years of knowledge and experience. We simply need to see retirement as an opportunity for growth and service; then our faith will be strengthened and our lives enriched. Never before has there been this much potential for church resources. At the turn of the century, not even one person out of twenty-five reached age sixty-five; now more than half do. And we are more vigorous than before too. In fact, the majority of those who attain sixty-five can expect to live into their eighties and beyond. That's a long time to quietly sit and rock on the front porch as Kenneth Chafin observed when his friend decided to unretire:

> My friend Kenneth Lawrence knew exactly what he would do when he retired from the railroad. He and his wife had bought a lot overlooking the fairway of a golf course in the beautiful Texas hill country. He planned to build a house, move from Houston and play golf every day. His golfing buddies who were years from retirement envied him.
>
> He had one small problem. At the time he retired, his wife Nelda, who was a professor at the University of Houston, had two more years to teach. Kenneth had good health, lots of energy, time on his hands and a pickup truck. Our church was helping relocate families from Vietnam and Cambodia, and someone enlisted Kenneth to collect furniture that members had donated for the apartments. He soon discovered that the refugees had a host of other needs, and he found delight in helping them learn how to live in their new country.
>
> When Nelda retired, they built their new home and moved to Kerrville, to what many thought was an ideal retirement. One Sunday, after they had been gone two years, I saw them in church and figured that they were just visiting. When I asked Kenneth, "How's the golf game?" he told me that they had put the new house up for sale and were moving back to Houston.
>
> "I discovered that playing golf with my friends every day wasn't as much fun as I had anticipated. And I realized that

> helping those Asian families start over was the most fulfilling experience of my life."

I guess that shouldn't have been such a surprise. After all, we were designed for God's work—wherever and whatever form it may take.

SIMPLICITY MADE SIMPLE

GET YOUR CHURCH OR PLACE OF WORSHIP TO HELP. Churches can help retirees see the importance of continuing service and provide the opportunities for it. If your church does not have a program that encourages seniors to be involved, consider starting one. Seniors can be challenged to serve as volunteers or to work for a modest honorarium. Seniors can enable congregations to fill positions and establish ministries that they could otherwise not afford. Even travel and other pursuits can be combined with Christian and other religious service. Retirement can be an exhilarating and liberating experience when it is a spiritual one as well.

CHECK OUT THESE THREE ONLINE RESOURCES to help you find a job. AARP publishes an annual list of the best employers for older workers in the hopes of encouraging more businesses to adopt "age-friendly policies and practices," such as flexible schedules and telecommuting. This year's list even included employers who allow workers to phase into retirement (and collect retirement benefits) while working part-time. Their site is www.aarp.org. Another site to check out is www.seniors4hire.org, which is aimed at helping older adults find employment. Many employers are placing a new emphasis on recruiting and hiring older workers including such companies as Bank of

America, Brinks, GNC, RadioShack, State Farm and Wells Fargo. Another good site is www.retiredbrains.com, where retirees can post résumés and search job listings.

DO SOME EXPLORING FIRST. You will find a career two ways: First, by seeking out the ideas of retirees currently or recently employed. Second, by researching the best employers in your community. Talk with those who are working now. Talk to them at church or where you worship, civic clubs and social events. Listen to what they like about working in retirement. Listen to comments about pay scales, younger bosses, work schedules, work-related stress, office politics, respect from younger workers and reactions from family and friends. Some of this conversation might spark job-related ideas in you. These conversations will also give you insight into the best employers in your community. Look for employers who have hired a large population of retirees and fifty-plus workers; employers who are willing to adjust work-shifts to accommodate your lifestyle; and those who pay attention to the pace of the workplace. A rush-rush style might be frustrating for you.

Lord, I am convinced that there is a new purpose for my life, which I have not yet achieved. Please open doors for me in places where I can serve You with the gifts and talents that You have invested in me. Amen.

PART TWO

Simply Settled in Your Home

THERE ARE MANY REASONS that it may well be time to resize your home when you retire. You may want a smaller space or a larger one to share with extended family members. But keeping a house simply because it is the one you have always lived in is not necessarily the best choice. In this section, I will share many ideas designed to prompt you to analyze and decide what is best for your unique living situation. There are so many options during this phase of life that offer the prospect of adventure and ease, and there are many organizations available to assist you with making the transition to the new lifestyle you want to enjoy. You may want to renovate or relocate, but before making any conclusions about where you want to spend all of—or the rest of—your retirement years, do read these next pages.

To Move or Not to Move

That I may dwell in the house of the Lord
all the days of my life. . . .

—PSALM 27:4 (NIV)

Have you ever dreamed about retirement? I know I have. In my retirement dreams, I am living on a little sailboat in the Caribbean waters off the coast of Tortola in the British Virgin Islands. I have fortunate friends who have spent their retirement winters there. Up until two years ago, when our friend Edward died, I had an open invitation for nearly thirty years to spend as much time as I desired in his family's little bungalow overlooking Cane Garden Bay. I love it there as much as his family did. Unfortunately, I am not sure that my husband shares that dream of living on a sailboat. Oh well . . . perhaps I can convince him to spend three months a year on my favorite little island. That seems like a nice compromise. But at this point, future retirement at my favorite island also seems extremely intangible. To move or not to move is more complicated than ever.

We baby boomers are facing a compounded decision regarding moving: today's workforce is working longer than ever before, our parents are also living longer and we are as concerned about relocating our elderly parents as we are with our own relocation. Housing decisions, such as selling, buying or renting have significant financial and well-being implications.

To move or not to move, when it comes to retirement, is an enormous decision. Many people have dreamed of moving to their favorite vacation spot only to find themselves bored or unhappy with their year-round supposed paradise. What seemed like a great idea in the beginning soon fizzles. My in-laws lasted only two years in Florida before they moved back north because they were lonely. One of the more popular new ideas seems to be moving to a nearby resort-style retirement community. In our neighboring state of New Jersey, there are several new communities that allow native New Yorkers to feel like they have moved to a resort while still being close enough to visit family and friends for the day, if they choose. Even here in Lancaster County, Pennsylvania, we have several large retirement communities that many New Jersey natives have moved to.

Aging in place is another growing trend. Many of us simply don't want to move for a variety of reasons. My mother's decision to stay put was partly determined by the fact that she has two dogs. Her yard is fenced so it is easy for her to open the door and let the dogs run. If she moved to a condominium (one that allowed dogs, of course), she would have to walk the dogs. Her life is busy enough; it simply didn't make sense to relocate, especially considering that she lives in the Snowbelt region of Ohio. The last thing our family needs to worry about is my mother slipping on the ice because the dogs tugged too hard on their leashes.

Many people think the best move is one that brings the older generation closer to their grown children. The reality is that just because you are parent and child does not mean that you will be best friends. Besides, as we work longer, many of us are starting second careers that often include a move—leaving an aged parent in a strange town with little social support. I read about an elderly gal who moved from her Southern city in the East to California in order to be close to her son and his family. Within six months her son had been transferred to New York. At first, she was scared and considered moving with them. But the thought of another move seemed overwhelming. So she decided to make this new community her home. It took a little time, but she did make good friends and is very happy she stayed.

Thousands of us are considering "rightsizing" to new quarters that will better fit our lifestyle. About half of my interior design clients are downsizing, while the other half are actually upsizing. Why would you upsize? There are a couple of good reasons: you have a large extended family that visits often, or because your accountant recommended that you take out a larger mortgage for the tax benefits. That is exactly why one of my clients chose to build a bigger nest. In fact, this individual has also purchased a second home as well for the same reason.

YOUR HOUSE SHOULD WORK FOR YOU

I read about another family in the September/October 2005 issue of *AARP The Magazine* who was trying to decide what to do about their home and mortgage. At age sixty and planning to retire in three years, they still had $50,000 left on their mortgage. They were wondering whether they should take money out of savings and pay off the mortgage—eliminating any further interest payments. They consulted with a financial adviser who pointed out that since they were nearing the end of their loan, they were paying more principal than interest. In fact, they were paying less than $3,000 a year in interest, which was not enough to push their deductible expenses above the standard deduction for couples. In other words, they were no longer getting any tax benefit from their mortgage. Until I gave it further thought, one strategy that was suggested to them surprised me. The couple had cash flow concerns as they approached retirement. Their financial adviser suggested they increase their mortgage loan and invest the extra borrowed funds. Following his advice, they took out a ten-year interest-only mortgage for $125,000, paid off the $50,000 old mortgage balance, and invested the remaining $75,000 in tax-free municipal bonds. Their monthly mortgage payments went up from $550 to $625, but their taxes decreased since they could deduct $7,500 in interest payments and $3,000 in property taxes, plus more for charitable deductions. Obviously, not everyone is comfortable with going into more debt. But it is an interesting option.

Before deciding to sell or move, Helen Barakauskas, senior real estate specialist with Prestige Properties in Connecticut, recommends thoroughly discussing with clients a full financial evaluation, including investment objectives, equity-conversion strategies, capital gains taxes and the other implications of selling. She says, "More importantly, perhaps, is a less-formal lifestyle analysis. I find out what is most difficult about their situation now and what is easier," she says. "If the current home is too costly to maintain and its style is difficult for comfortable living, that's important."

"Sometimes, the various assessments indicate that seniors needn't move at all," says Dennis Kaiser, a senior specialist with ReMax Associates in San Diego. He also says, "Often a reverse mortgage will enable them to stay where they are, and to many, that's very important." Sally Hurme, a consumer-protection attorney with AARP, agrees. She says, "You can make needed modifications in the home and generate the cash needed to assist you."

To move or not to move? It's a big decision—but it can also be an exciting opportunity that can lead to new adventures. We must all remember that this earthly home is just that—an earthly home. God has amazing mansions in heaven waiting for all of us. In the meantime, tuck your treasured memories in your heart as Marilyn Morgan Helleberg did when she decided to make the big move:

> This house has been our home for eighteen years, but now that our children are all grown, we don't need this much space anymore. Last night I mentioned to John, who has recently moved into a place of his own, that we're thinking of selling the house. His face clouded over. "But, Mom, Rusty's buried here, and . . . and think of all the marshmallows we've roasted in that fireplace . . . and what about the long talks we've had together, sitting on the deck after school?"
>
> I understood how he felt. I remember going to my old hometown after Mother moved out of the family house, and realizing that I'd never be able to go home again. It's a sad feeling. And yet, an ending is also a beginning. John and I joined hands and thanked God that all of those wonderful things that make a house a home are not in the house itself but in our hearts. We'll take them with us into our new beginnings! I hope John can hold onto that, through all the endings and beginnings, the good-byes and hellos, the uprootings and replantings of his life. I hope I can too.

EVALUATE YOUR LIFESTYLE AND YOUR NEEDS. Start with the basics—do you need to be close to public transportation? How important is it to be near quality medical care and family and friends? How important is security? Although it may be difficult leaving home, retirement communities can help some seniors make new friends and discover new activities. A communal living situation, where residents share one meal a day with others, encourages social contact and cuts down on the loneliness that especially plagues single seniors.

A CONDOMINIUM CAN BE A GREAT OPTION—but not everyone has the right personality to fit in. Community condos have "boards" that decide what everyone can and cannot do. One friend of mine found it nearly impossible to live with her condo's association rules. She could not have a bird feeder; she could not plant her own flowers. Her granddaughter was not allowed to ride her bike in most of the public area. In fact, the community would have been happier not to have her granddaughter ever visit. Not every condo situation is like my friend's, but be sure to talk to several residents before making a choice to live in a controlled senior condominium community.

Find a great place to live, but **TAKE IT ONE STEP AT A TIME**. Before selling your house and moving to paradise, consider keeping your home and renting a place for a year first. This will help you to make an intelligent decision later about real estate values and locations while you decide for certain that paradise year-round is really right for you. If you don't yet know where your earthly paradise is located, check out the Retirement Living Information Center for outstanding places to retire. Their Web site is www.retirementliving.com. They have information on cities and communities all around the country. The site provides material on recreation, arts and culture, education, senior programs, medical facilities, airports and weather along with a brief history of each community.

BE SURE YOU KNOW BEFORE YOU GO. Is the climate comfortable year-round? Will you be able to make friends easily? Is the area served by a major airline and a good health facility? Are there opportunities for part-time work or volunteer work fitting your particular interests and hobbies? Have you spent enough time in the community to know it is really what you want?

REFIT TO STAY PUT. Start with the outside of your home. Will the façade require constant upkeep? How's your landscaping? If possible, do repairs while you are still working and have more flexibility with your cash flow. Could you construct a ramp to the front door if you needed to? How many steps do you have inside and out? Make sure that all stairwells are well lit and have sturdy handrails. Are your doorways at least thirty-six inches wide to accommodate a wheelchair if necessary? Eliminate plush carpeting and install laminate or hardwood floors to make walking easier. Be sure your bathroom can be readapted to be suitable for a handicapped person. My mom completely remodeled her bathroom and installed grab bars, an easy-to-get-into tub and a higher toilet. We also enlarged the doorway to the hallway to make room for a walker or wheelchair. Mom added an insulated door to close off the upstairs bedrooms in order to save money on heating and cooling.

Father, Your Word says that you know the exact places Your people will live. Please give me the wisdom to either move or remain where I am in order to stay in Your perfect plan for my life. Amen.

A Wise Move

During the night Pharaoh summoned Moses and Aaron
and said, "Up! Leave my people, you and the Israelites!
Go, worship the Lord as you have requested.
Take your flocks and herds, as you have said, and go. . . ."

—EXODUS 12:31–32 (NIV)

Can you imagine someone coming to your home in the middle of the night and telling you it was time to move *NOW*! The Israelites had been living in Egypt for over four hundred years. Yes, they were slaves, but they had not always been enslaved. Their life and history was entrenched in Egypt. Although they knew they were going to the Promised Land, the move was still incredibly difficult. The Israelites wandered through the deserts of Negev and Sinai for forty years before moving north to settle in Canaan's fertile areas. The fierce desert wind would blow westward, drying up the Judean air. Occasional rain, a little grass here and there but mostly just dry desert sand is what they faced. Overall, their moving experience was not a good one.

Unlike the Israelites, your move to the "promised land" can be a little easier with some organization and planning. Although making the decision to move can be especially difficult for seniors, the decision and the moving process is made considerably easier if we plan ahead and enlist the help of professionals.

Obviously, choosing to move on your own when you are healthy and independent will make the transition from your long-term home to an apartment or community much smoother. If you fear growing older and not being able to care for yourself, or if you are a caregiver concerned about the safety of another senior and feel unable to continue to provide the necessary care at home, then let me assure you that moving is the right decision, despite the fact that it can be difficult and complicated.

Along with death and divorce, the process of moving rates high on the stress meter. No matter how prepared we think we are to deal with a move, most of us react more emotionally than we thought we would. The older we get, the more overwhelming the entire experience can be. Rocky Welkowitz, a licensed realtor and founder of "Moving Solutions for Seniors," helps seniors deal with the emotional burdens, even trauma, of moving out of a home that is filled with most of their life's memories. She says, "I love my work because you can do so much to help people. I have been able to make life easier and happier for a lot of people."

Welkowitz's organization is just one of many such companies around the country that specialize in moving seniors. Her crew at Moving Solutions sorts, packs, moves and unpacks furniture and belongings for their clients. One client, Bill Coy, was emotionally paralyzed. After his wife died his health problems made taking care of their home of thirty-three years nearly impossible. His daughter Sandy recalls, "He just basically sat there and did nothing. The house was falling apart around him." But Coy, now eighty, was truly overwhelmed by the thought of moving.

Welkowitz and her crew came to the rescue. They sold his house in ten days and had him moved and situated in his new home in no time at all. "When he walked into the new place, everything was in the drawers . . . the bed was made, the pictures were on the wall," his daughter said. "He basically walked from his house into a setup apartment." Now that's the way to handle a move.

Moving is rarely an enjoyable experience. But for senior citizens, it can be especially draining. Seniors may be mourning the loss of a spouse or leaving a home of fifty years. Sorting and packing possessions is physically and emotionally demanding. Often family live too far away to help. Hiring a professional group that specializes in understanding the difficulties associated with such a process and such a vulnerable clientele can make a big difference. Welkowitz has a crew of seven independent contractors that includes homemakers, a retired teacher, a geriatric nurse and an artist/decorator. She charges an average hourly rate of thirty dollars. Her crew will supervise the movers and sort belongings, even selling some at auction and donating others to charity, if desired. When they finish, all a client has left to do is arrive in the new home.

GIVE YOURSELF TIME TO ADJUST

Once we do arrive in our new home or apartment, we will still have some emotional adjusting to do. Even if we have just moved into our dream homes, we will still find some tugging on our heartstrings. Elsie Bischoff, eighty-three, says that parting with the home and furniture she had shared with her husband "was the hardest thing for me." In addition to stirring up emotions, moving into a retirement community presents practical and logistical problems. For example, if you are moving to smaller quarters or moving in with family, it means you must decide which possessions to discard and which to keep. Being able to take along some family treasures, furniture and mementos of significance can help make the transition easier.

When one of my clients became a widow, she decided to move into a small addition on her daughter's home. We purposely chose her most treasured items and furnishings to go with her so that it would feel like home. It also helped her to keep an emotional connection to her husband. Three years later, she called me because she wanted to redecorate. Those three years gave her the time she needed to grieve and recover. Now she was ready to start her new life—and she wanted new furniture to go with it!

Guideposts writer Phyllis Hobe wrote about how she learned to wait patiently for her stepfather after his move:

> When my stepfather came to live with me a few years ago, he was quite depressed. Although he realized he couldn't go on living alone, he missed the home he had known for so many years. Whenever his friends called to see how he was, he would always say the same thing: "I never got a chance to go back home. I just went into the hospital and then I came here."
>
> I thought my dad's sadness would go away, but when it didn't, I spoke to our family doctor about it. "Be patient," the doctor told me. "He needs more time. When we get older, it takes longer to feel comfortable in new places." I never said

anything to Dad; I just kept on trying to make him feel welcome. But sometimes when I saw loneliness in his eyes, I thought my heart was going to break.

A few weeks ago, my dad and I went to a christening and a reception. We were away a full day, and when we came home my dad stood quietly at the back door while I fumbled for my keys. "You know," he said, "I had a good time—but it's good to be home!" He was looking around at all the trees and smiling, as if he owned the place. And there wasn't a bit of loneliness in his eyes. Our doctor was right. My dad just needed more time to make himself at home.

SIMPLICITY MADE SIMPLE

Take time to make a plan. When my clients are moving, we always **START BY DRAWING UP A FLOOR PLAN** of their new spaces. Then we go through the house and decide what is going to the new location, what will be sold or donated and what will be discarded. We label each piece of furniture with the name of the room in which it will be placed. As their belongings are packed, we label each box, carefully indicating on the box the contents and the room location as well. Fragile items are marked accordingly and placed together so that they are handled gently. Anything that requires very specific packing or more attention in moving is delegated either to a professional service or handled directly by the homeowners so that they know it is safe. For years, I also provided a picture hanging and accessory placing service. Clients loved this.

HIRE A SENIOR-SPECIALIST MOVING FIRM. One way to guarantee that your move goes well is to enlist the help of professionals who specialize in moving seniors. Look for companies that are part of NASMM, the National Association of Senior Move Managers. Moving professionals can provide support and assistance with both the physical and emotional aspects of the moving process. They can assess and perform the important steps in the moving process including planning and customizing floor plans; referring realtors, movers, shippers, liquidators and charitable organizations; contacting utilities; packing, unpacking, organizing, settling and decorating. Utilizing the help of a professional move manager or moving company will cost money, but it can alleviate the stress and frustration of moving.

Lord, when it is time for me to make changes in my lifestyle, please give me the grace to enjoy the newness You want to bring to my life. Amen.

Need a Little Assistance?

Moreover I said unto the king, If it please the king,
let letters be given me to the governors beyond the river,
that they may convey me over till I come into Judah;
And a letter unto Asaph the keeper of the king's forest,
that he may give me timber to make beams for the gates
of the palace which appertained to the house,
and for the wall of the city, and for the house
that I shall enter into. And the king granted me,
according to the good hand of my God upon me.

—NEHEMIAH 2:7–8 (KJV)

After praying about it, Nehemiah asked the king for permission to go to Judea. As soon as he got a positive answer, he began asking for additional help. Sadly, sometimes when we have needs, we hesitate to ask others for help because we are afraid to approach them or perhaps we are simply afraid of admitting that we are not as able as we once were. Nehemiah was smart; he went directly to the person who could help him the most. The lesson here is not to be reluctant to ask those who are most able to help. God's answer to your prayers may come as a result of asking others for help.

This is especially true as we age. Being a good steward is not just about money, but also about planning realistically for our future physical needs as well. At one time, families simply took care of each other as they aged. Today, many families need two incomes, which makes it nearly impossible to care for an aging loved one without some help. The good news is that there are more options today than ever before, from adult day care and in-home service providers to independent-living facilities, assisted living and continuing care retirement communities.

Adult day care meets caregiving needs at many levels. Hugh Downs, the TV news host, wrote extensively about the benefits of adult day care in his book, *Fifty to Forever*. Downs said, "Adult day care is a precious resource for family members and friends who are providing various levels of care."[8] Adult day care provides the opportunity for the caregiver to live a fairly normal life, including the ability to continue working during the day knowing that a loved one is safe. Though services vary from one community to another, they all share a common philosophy, which rests on three key points. First, according to the National Institute on Adult Daycare, these programs salute individuality of participants and recognize their strengths, weaknesses and potential for growth. Second, they take a holistic approach to the needs of the participants. They also recognize an interrelationship among the physical, social, emotional and environmental aspects of real well-being. Third, they seek to create an environment that will encourage a positive self-image for those in their care.

In-home service programs offer another alternative that might just be right for you or a loved one. Most in-home service agencies offer a variety of homemaker services such as light housekeeping, meal preparation and running errands, as well as individual care with personal hygiene, including bathing and dressing. The best part of this kind of service is that it provides those who wish to remain in their own home with a safe and viable way of doing so.

But there is a lot to consider when choosing an agency because not all states require licensing for home care agencies. Here in Lancaster, the Pennsylvania Home Care Association has been attempting to get such licensure for over ten years. They suggest that you make sure that periodic criminal background checks are required for all home care employees. You will feel much more at ease knowing that your loved one is receiving care from someone who is completely trustworthy.

Also ensure that proper training is provided for new employees and is ongoing. Make sure this training is under the direction of a registered nurse and that competencies are required. Also be sure that the agency has a nurse doing an assessment and developing a detailed plan of care in conjunction with you and your loved one who will be receiving the care.

ACCEPT ASSISTANCE AS A GIFT FROM GOD

Continuing care retirement communities (CCRCs) seem to be the way of the future because they can provide a full spectrum of care and services, allowing residents to move into an assisted-living unit and progressing to a nursing home, all in the same place. Many of my retiring clients have chosen this kind of arrangement. Willow Valley Retirement Community, here in Lancaster, is one of the most respected in the country. It draws retirees from all over the country. I think it is so popular because it is not only surrounded by some of the most beautiful countryside, but it has also put together an amazing array of complementary programs such as a spa, a cultural center that attracts great entertainers, a golf course, art programs, eight restaurants, a banquet facility, and a state-of-the-art exercise facility as well as an excellent medical staff and supportive living services. In addition, it has over eighty-five different floor plans to choose from. Willow Valley, like most CCRCs, has a menu of services that it provides. The Lifecare contract includes a residential nursing team, skilled nursing, assisted living and memory support.

Ultimately, we will all have to face the changing reality of our physical and mental situation. Examining our options before we need them is a good way to be prepared and make our decision easier when the time comes. The hardest part can simply be accepting that we are not as young as we once were, and a little help can go a long way, as writer Eleanor Sass discovered:

> Several years ago, I developed a hand tremor. It has since been diagnosed as a mild case of Parkinson's disease. Most of the time, medication keeps it under control. But when I am tense or worried, the tremor can get out of control.
>
> The other day, I went to the post office for stamps. The lines for postal-worker service were enormous, so I decided to use one of the stamp machines. Since I was holding envelopes in my left hand, with no place to set them down, it was difficult to keep the bills flat as I tried to feed them into the machine with my right hand. The machine kept rejecting them with the notation "Be sure your bills are flat." After several tries, I became aware that a line was forming behind me.

Then I heard a pleasant female voice say, "Would you like for me to do that for you?"

I cringed. *Someone is watching me*, I thought. *Now I'll never get these bills into the machine!*

In my retirement years I find that I'm deeply sensitive to offers for help with things that I could do all by myself just ten years ago. As I turned to answer the woman, a still small voice seemed to say, *Let her help you.* So instead of muttering something like, "Thank you, but no thanks," I said, "Yes, please." She stepped forward and within ten seconds I had my stamps.

As we left the post office, I thanked the young woman and briefly explained my problem. "That's okay," she answered, "I understand."

Ever since, I never hesitate to accept help when I need it. It's what God wants me to do.

SIMPLICITY MADE SIMPLE

MAKE THE RIGHT CHOICE for adult day care. Traditionally, adult day care programs fall into two categories: medically based and social/recreationally based. In medically based facilities, nurses may provide supervision and counseling for health problems. Most of these programs are actually housed in a hospital or nursing home. They maintain communication with the participant's family and personal physician. They can also provide therapy services such as occupational therapy and speech therapy. This is especially good for stroke victims. Community-based facilities have nurses, aides and other professionals on staff for general supervision but they do not offer rehabilitation services. Many will provide daily blood pressure checks and other procedures to track general health but are primarily there to meet the social and recreational needs of participants. Most also provide a substantial hot meal each day.

FIND AN AGENCY WITH COMPASSION. When it comes to choosing an in-home service provider, be sure they focus on hiring those with compassion. No matter how many safety policies are implemented by an agency, the quality of care will suffer if administered by aides who fail to show compassion for their senior clients. Your loved one deserves to receive care from someone who is kind, respectful, understanding and knowledgeable of his or her special needs. It is also important to inquire about the range of services the agency will provide, and if you need individualized service, find out whether the agency will be flexible enough to meet your special needs. Also, ask how long the agency has been in business. Experience is a necessary quality and an agency's record will put you at ease when making your decision. Also, be certain to consider the turnover rate of the staff. An agency that has a revolving door of in-home aides may have some internal problems that could affect the level of service you receive.

CAREFULLY CONSIDER HOW TO PAY FOR SERVICES. The good news is that in most areas, assisted living costs half as much as nursing home care. The bad news is that nine out of ten residents in assisted living are paying for it themselves. According to the Assisted Living Federation of America, the idea that Medicare will pay for assisted living or nursing home care is a popular misconception. Medicaid may pay for some assistance, but you will either have to be poor or spend down your assets to that level in order to qualify.

Typical assisted living residence costs are anywhere from $620 a month to $995, on the low side. On the high end, they range from $1,639 a month to $3,565. Nursing homes are about $4,000 per month or $48,000 a year. In a CCRC, residents pay a lump sum at the beginning or perhaps a combination of up-front costs and monthly payments. The entrance fee can be as low as $30,000 or as high as $500,000. The monthly fees range from $500 to $2,000 a month. One of the most obvious ways to afford your retirement care is simply to sell your home, if you have one. That is what most of my clients have done who have moved into Willow Valley. Another option is a reverse mortgage. This is a good idea if you are planning to stay in your home and hire in-home help, but it makes no sense if you are planning to move to assisted living or a CCRC. Long-term care insurance is an option for baby boomers and others who wish to plan for possible needs in the future.

EVALUATE ALL YOUR OPTIONS when it comes to choosing assisted living residences. The Assisted Living Federation of America has a guide that can help you ask the right questions. You can call them at (703) 691-8100 or access their Web site www.alfa.org. They recommend that you consider the atmosphere of the facility through the eyes of the person who will be living there. Watch to see how your loved one reacts when he or she meets the staff and other residents. Is the décor welcoming and homelike? Do the current residents appear to be compatible with your loved one? Will the particular personality, culture and ambience of that setting support the physical, emotional and spiritual needs of the prospective resident? The answer to that question is critical in determining the success of your loved one's choice. It is also suggested that you make several return visits to the residence at the top of your list in order to experience the staff in a variety of situations.

Forgive me, Lord, for times that I refuse Your help because of my stubborn pride. Help me to see this phase of needing assistance as a time to make new friends and develop deeper connections with the friends I already have. Amen.

Alternate Living—What's Your Pleasure?

By faith he sojourned in the land of promise,
as in a strange country, dwelling in tabernacles
with Isaac and Jacob, the heirs with him of the
same promise: For he looked for a city which hath
foundations, whose builder and maker is God.

—HEBREWS 11:9–10 (KJV)

Hebrews makes much of the fact that the patriarchs lived in tents. Apparently, they saw themselves as temporary visitors rather than permanent residents on this earth. They kept their eyes fixed on their true homeland, "the city with foundations, whose architect and builder is God." We all know that Abraham's life was filled with faith. He was willing at God's command to leave home and go to another land—obeying without question. As we think about retirement and what it might be for any of us, we should not be surprised if God asks us to give up our secure and familiar surroundings to carry out His will.

Perhaps it's not so surprising then that a growing number of seniors are joining the Peace Corps. In fact, the Peace Corps is actively reaching out to seniors. "Older people bring skills and life experience to the foreign country they serve, where many times age is respected," says Edwin Jorge, the Peace Corps's New York regional manager.

For years, volunteers over age fifty represented just one percent of the Peace Corps's ranks. But in recent years, the number of fifty-plus volunteers has jumped to six percent of the total of 7,733 members, according to the Peace Corps's Web site (www.peacecorps.gov). Serving in the Peace Corps may be an ideal option for those who aren't satisfied with "traditional volunteer roles" and who seek the "spirit of adventure" that prevails in the Corps.

There are very few requirements to volunteer: You must be a U.S. citizen and able to meet certain medical guidelines, but these standards are no problem for older Americans in relatively good health. One young retiree, age fifty-seven, of Hershey, Pennsylvania, said, "There are few volunteers my age but my young colleagues have helped me reconnect with the sparks of my youth. I have great respect for them." He does, however, feel that his age and slight loss of hearing put him at a disadvantage in mastering a new language. He added that he needed extra tutoring to learn Spanish well enough to communicate with Nicaraguans, the kind of help anyone with language difficulties gets.

If the Peace Corps doesn't sound like your cup of tea, how about cruising? I'm not just talking about taking a two-week vacation cruise but actually living on a cruise ship! I'm not kidding. Living on a cruise ship provides a better quality of life and is cost effective for older adults who need help to live independently, according to a recent study published in the *Journal of the American Geriatrics Society*. People older than sixty-five who enjoy travel and have good cognitive function, but need some help in daily living, are ideal candidates for care on a cruise ship.

According to the study, the typical resident in a U.S. assisted-living facility is an eighty-year-old widowed, white, ambulatory woman who needs help with about two activities of daily living, such as bathing, toileting, feeding, dressing and transfers (for example, from bed to a chair). Many older adults may in fact do better on a cruise ship, at a similar cost, even for many years. Lee Lindquist, a physician and instructor of medicine at Northwestern University in Illinois, compared the amenities and costs in assisted-living facilities with accommodations on cruise ships. Cruise ships have superior health facilities—one or more doctors, nurses available twenty-four hours a day, defibrillators, equipment for dealing with medical emergencies and the ability to give intravenous fluids and antibiotics. The authors calculated that the long-term cost for a person to live on a cruise ship from the age of eighty until his or her death would be $230,497, compared with $228,075 for a U.S. assisted-living facility. Where would you rather live?

YOU CAN FINALLY SEE THE WORLD

Perhaps you've always dreamed of living abroad? Friends of mine have been vacationing annually in Scotland for nearly a decade. They now spend almost two months a year renting a house there. They will ultimately make Scotland their home when they retire. The lure to exotic places is strong for many retirees. In 1997 there were more than 360,000 Americans living abroad in retirement.

Living abroad has many advantages, and retiring abroad can save you big bucks. Jane Parker, coauthor of *Adventures Abroad*, estimates that in some cases a couple can enjoy foreign retirement living at one-third to one-half of what it costs to live in the States. According to her study, comfortable living in Mexico could cost $1,000 to $1,200 a month, and living in Portugal costs $1,800 to $2,000 a month. "For this you get a one-thousand to twenty-five hundred square foot home in a middle-class neighborhood, enjoy fresh food from open-air markets and local delicacies from restaurants, and attend plays and concerts for less than ten dollars each."

Seniors Home Exchange is another simple and very affordable way to try living in another country temporarily. For seventy-nine dollars you get a three-year subscription to the only home exchange program designed exclusively for the over-fifty age group. Seniors Home Exchange provides a directory as a source of reference only. You simply choose a country and make arrangements with one of the subscribers to exchange your home with theirs for as long as you like. All arrangements are made privately by the individual parties. You choose with whom you want to exchange homes. You can visit their Web site for more information at www.seniorshomeexchange.com.

There are no limitations. You are free to make arrangements for as many exchanges as you desire. Since most subscribers no longer have young children to care for, they are more flexible and are able to exchange at various times of the year. It's an ideal way for visitors to experience the lifestyle of a country, with the friends and neighbors of the exchange partners often happy to recommend local attractions, shops and restaurants well away from the expensive tourist trail.

Many exchanges include cars. This represents an enormous savings on rental and insurance expenses. You can also save on food by cooking instead of spending your entire budget eating out every day. The exchange is not limited to just conventional homes either; they also include motor homes. A home exchange, in short, is an effective and economical way to truly experience different cultures as they really are—from a home, not a hotel room. That makes it a remarkable experience.

Another way to see the world is simply to travel. Elderhostel and ElderTreks are two groups that specialize in adventure and educational travel for people over fifty. Elderhostel (www.elderhostel.org) is America's first and the world's largest educational travel organization. They are a nonprofit group that provides exceptional learning adventures to nearly two hundred thousand older adults every year. They offer over ten thousand programs a year in more than ninety countries. From Paris to Delhi, Elderhostel has unique educational experience opportunities infused with a spirit of camaraderie and adventure that can enrich and enhance your life. Their experts share stimulating information through in-depth lectures, field trips and cultural excursions that can broaden your perspective. If you've always dreamed of learning to paint, you can do so with Elderhostel on Nantucket Island. You can even study literature in London. The best part of their programs is that they are all-inclusive in cost. They include all meals, lectures, field trips, cultural excursions, gratuities and medical or insurance coverage.

ElderTreks is an organization that caters to those fifty and over looking for adventure. They have been around for over twenty-five years, specializing in creating memorable travel adventures to exotic locations in more than sixty countries and on every continent. All itineraries at ElderTreks stress cultural interaction, close contact with local people, exploration of the natural world, physical activity and sustainable travel. You can learn more about them at their Web site www.eldertreks.com.

I like the fact that they keep the groups small. In fact, they guarantee that no group for any of its land adventures will be larger than sixteen people.

One person in each party must be at least fifty years old, but companions of any age may join them. I think this would be a wonderful vacation to take with your grandchildren. Prices range from under $2,000 to $5,000, and the activity level runs the gamut from "gentle" to "demanding." You simply choose your preference.

SIMPLICITY MADE SIMPLE

SOMETIMES THE BEST MOVE IS RIGHT DOWNTOWN. Fifty-plus empty nesters are beginning to abandon sprawling suburbs for pedestrian-friendly cities, towns, and planned communities where they can walk, not drive, to offices and shops. According to the U.S. Census figures, "The upper end of the downtown condo market is largely boomers," says John McIlwain, a senior fellow at the Urban Land Institute in Washington, D.C. But the foot traffic is not limited to big cities. Town centers ringed with housing are popping up in close-in suburbs and new urbanist, master-planned communities too. Dan Burden, director of the advocacy group Walkable Communities, Inc., has assembled a list of twelve requirements to determine how walkable a community is. Visit his Web site for more information: www.walkable.org. His essentials include a lively, compact town center with a good mix of stores; tree-lined, low-speed streets; and public space (a park or plaza) within seven hundred feet of a home. "Look for places that put people first, cars second," Burden says.

FOLLOW THE ADVICE FROM THE U.S. STATE DEPARTMENT when you travel. Fill out the emergency information page of your passport and make two copies of your passport identification page. Take one copy with you and leave one at home with friends or family. If your passport is lost or stolen, having a copy will facilitate replacement. Also, be sure to leave a copy of your itinerary with family or friends too. If you plan to stay abroad for more than two weeks, check in with the U.S. Embassy in the country you are visiting as soon as you arrive. You may notify the embassy by phone or register in person. This will expedite communication in case someone contacts the embassy looking for you. My mother has a friend now living in Israel. There have been two separate occasions when it was necessary for Mom to contact the embassy to locate her friend about an emergency situation.

EVALUATE BEFORE YOU MOVE ABROAD. Before you decide to retire abroad, consider the same factors you would in evaluating locations in the United States, including affordability, incidence of crime, comfort level of the climate, good health care and accessibility to cultural and consumer amenities. A good way to examine life in another country is by living there in an exchange home. Try exchanging homes several times, in different seasons. Exercise caution if you plan to buy a home abroad. There are many rules and regulations for living and buying property in each country. For example, if you are interested in buying a fashionable home in a London neighborhood, you will most likely be buying your home with a long-term lease. In the West End section, the land is actually owned by the Duke of Westminster and his family, so when you buy a home you must also consider future costs for renewal of the lease. Mortgages also vary and can be challenging. In some countries, you can only finance fifty percent. Oftentimes, the rate is not fixed—the rate of interest floats with the interest rate changes. In Spain and Italy, for example, mortgages for foreigners are nonexistent, so you must pay cash.

Take it easy on yourself. To **MINIMIZE RISK OF HEALTH TROUBLE AWAY FROM HOME**, follow these precautions. Before confirming your reservations, be sure your need for bathroom trips is not too demanding. Visit your doctor and dentist before your trip. Schedule your appointments far enough in advance. I just prevailed on my mother to make all her doctor appointments three months in advance of our January vacation. If you are being treated for an ongoing medical condition, carry copies of your medical records with you. Medicare recipients who need supplemental travel health insurance for travel outside the United States should contact either their insurance provider or AARP Insurance Division at (800) 523-5800 for further information. Also, be sure to pace yourself as you travel. Get adequate sleep—fatigue aggravates existing medical conditions. Rest once or twice a day. The ancient ruins will still be there when you wake up from your nap!

Lord, I am excited about the possibility of new adventures now that there is more time to enjoy them. Please give me the wisdom to maintain a healthy life in order to enjoy Your wonderful world. Amen.

Multigenerational Living

Then Joseph said to his brothers and to his father's household,
"I will go up and speak to Pharaoh and will say to him,
'My brothers and my father's household, who were
living in the land of Canaan, have come to me.'"

—GENESIS 46:31 (NIV)

Joseph's father's house included at least seventy-one people—wives, sons, daughters-in-law and grandchildren—when the patriarch entered Egypt. In Old Testament times, the household was the basic unit of society. Although my family was not quite as large as this one, we did have several generations living under the same roof.

Just yesterday, my mother, sister and niece were discussing the possibility of all of them living together at Mom's house. It's certainly feasible and a good option for the three of them. My niece is young, still working on her college degree. My sister has been a single mom for twenty years and is very close to my mother. It certainly would make things financially and physically easier for all of them. Mom loves to cook, as does my niece. My sister is good at all kinds of housework and repair. They get along well enough and the house actually has three levels. So it's conceivable that they could each have a separate floor, which would allow them each a sense of privacy.

FIND GRACE FOR ANY NEW PLACE

When we think about multigenerational living, most of us simply think only about having an elderly relative or friend move in with us because they need special care. But today there is a whole new kind of multigenerational family to consider: grandparents who are raising their grandchildren. "Grandfamilies," as they are called, were 2.4 million strong in 2002 and growing.

As I watched the news regarding Hurricane Katrina, they spotlighted one such family. The grandparents have custody of their six young grandchildren, ages one through eleven. They evacuated from Louisiana to Alabama and now are faced with the legal issue that Alabama doesn't recognize their custody order. Clearly, these grandfamilies require special considerations.

It's also creating some interesting challenges when it comes to building communities for the elderly. Sharon West, director of the Buffalo Municipal Housing Authority, says, "The dynamics of families are changing, and we need to figure out new ways to address it so these children can grow up whole." West should know because she is raising her own six-year-old granddaughter. The results are new homes with services and features for all members of these families.

Developers in Detroit are planning two projects of specially designed low-income housing. There's day care for the children and windows that look out over the playground so the grandparents can watch from inside. Other cities with plans for grandfamily housing include Baltimore; New Haven,

Connecticut; Cleveland; Philadelphia; Phoenix; Oklahoma City; Trenton, New Jersey; Nashville; Sacramento; and Tacoma, Washington. The community in Detroit will include a library, computer room, classroom and recreation center among other built-in conveniences. The apartments in Boston are being built to accommodate both age groups, with grab bars in the bathrooms and covers for the electrical outlets.

No matter the age of the generations, multigenerational living has positive and negative aspects. Hugh Downs says, "On the plus side, intergenerational living provides a sense of continuity for family, especially for extended family and grandchildren; my father knew his great-grandchildren as teenagers. On the minus side, even though you are now an adult, you may be relegated to the child's role again, particularly if your parent tends to be aggressive or domineering. For some people, the negatives will outweigh the positives. It is important to admit up front that this type of arrangement doesn't work for everyone."

Downs also says that if you are considering asking an elderly relative or friend to move in with you, be sure your motivation is more than simply a sense of "oughtness"—that is, if you are doing this only because you think you should, that may not be enough motivation to carry you through the next decade.

Architect Sarah Susanka, coauthor of *Inside the Not So Big House: Discovering the Details that Bring a Home to Life*, says, "Good design and clear communication make multigenerational households work for everyone." She also says we should remember that when we bring another generation into our home, they are our guests, and we have every right to define how we want them to engage in the life of our existing household.

I think we sometimes forget to define boundaries or perhaps we simply avoid it, especially if we have unresolved issues with our family members. Susanka recommends addressing your expectations right away by letting your new guest know that there will be a family meeting to review how things are going after a specified length of time—perhaps a couple of weeks or a month—where you will discuss what is and isn't working.

I can't say our family was perfect or that it was easy with four generations living together, but it did enrich our lives. I feel very blessed to have really known my great-grandmother and my grandmother. I think too that it gave all of us a perspective on life that could not have been taught any other way. Guideposts writer Drue Duke was also blessed by having her grandmother live with her family—and it made a difference in her life as well:

> Grandma lived with us all of my growing-up years. No one ever said it was easy for three generations to share one roof. We had our ups and downs; we kids found her old-fashioned notions ridiculous and she considered our newfangled ideas equally absurd.
>
> But it was not the generation gap between us that I remember most about Grandma. It was her total, unshakeable faith and confidence in us. I can still picture her, tilted back a bit to see better through her glasses, shaking her head with its small knot of white hair as she read the daily newspaper.
>
> "*Tch! Tch! Tch!*" was the sound her tongue made against her teeth anytime she read of juveniles in trouble. "I am so glad this is not your name here." And then those blue eyes would pierce straight into me. "Oh, but of course it couldn't be. You would never do anything so bad, like that."

And you know, she was right. I had my share of temptations, of course, but anytime I felt my resistance weakening where something really *bad* was concerned, Grandma's words would stop me. Somehow, there was no way I could bear to break her trust in me.

Today, I proudly bear the name of "Grandma," and I feel that same confidence in my two grandchildren. I keep reminding myself that I must make them aware of my trust in them. I must give it to them as a buoy to cling to when the going gets rough.

I think this might even be the biggest job God has for us grandparents to do.

SIMPLICITY MADE SIMPLE

Before moving in with any extended family, define your relationship. Hugh Downs suggests writing down your feelings to **DETERMINE YOUR LEVEL OF COMFORT** with that relationship. Be realistic. He warns us not to succumb to hazy images of media ideals like Aunt Bee on *The Andy Griffith Show*. We must face the facts. Downs asks: "Can you name three characteristics that you appreciate? Can you name three that annoy you? Which list was easier to create?" We also need to accept how we have handled conflict and stress in the past with this person. Has one of you been forceful and the other submissive? Has the pattern been one that bred resentment? Have you both been argumentative? Are you ready to handle conflict situations in your own home?

ACCEPT THE FACT THAT NOT EVERYONE CAN LIVE TOGETHER. Living together always requires work. Every family has its own particular characteristics—

and sometimes they make living together impossible. That does not mean that you are cruel or insensitive. It simply means that you are making the best decision possible under the circumstances—and that will be good for everyone.

INVOLVE THE WHOLE FAMILY. Bringing another family member into your home will change the dynamics. Your spouse and your children will need to understand what will be required of them. If your son is used to listening to his music after school each day, it could become a problem if Grandma doesn't think it's the kind of thing he should listen to. Everyone must be in agreement and accept the full responsibility that will be needed to make this arrangement work. You won't be able to avoid all conflicts, but if you prepare in advance and set guidelines early on to determine how you will handle conflicts, you will be much further ahead.

BE REALISTIC about your own life and its flexibility. What are your present responsibilities? Which of these cannot be altered for any reason? Which are negotiable? If your life is ordered in such a way that you cannot take on this additional responsibility, then say so. Consider your own health. Do you have a physical or emotional condition that could be compromised by adding stress and strain to it? Most importantly, do you have a good sense of humor? In caring for my granddad, humor is what got both Mom and Dad through the hard times.

Everyone needs his or her own "tent." Privacy is partially spatial and partly psychological. **PEOPLE NEED TO FEEL A SENSE OF SEPARATION TO LIVE COMFORTABLY TOGETHER** without constantly *being* together. One old idea that is taking hold again is the "granny cottage." Once a popular way to keep family members close—but not too close—second units or granny cottages have nearly been "zoned" and "bylawed" to extinction in many areas. Now there are signs that they are making a comeback. "As our population ages, it will be invaluable for cities to let these kinds of units evolve," says Ann Daigle, Ventura, California's planning and urban development manager. People can add a granny unit in the backyard affordably because they already own the land beneath it. Besides granny cottages, building a few hundred extra feet as an addition can also make the difference that allows living together to be both reasonable and manageable for all considered. One family had a local architect design a twenty-by-twenty-four-foot addition for them. It gave grandma her own ground-level entrance off a small private garden space, and a single door from her space into the main house. Although she was literally right next door, the entire addition was designed to create a sense of separation and privacy. The door connecting the house and grandma's apartment looks like a front door—a clear visual sign that this is a different place with a different homeowner.

Lord, You make all things work together for our good, so if my family unit grows at a time when I thought it would decrease, I trust You for the grace to adjust. I want to be a blessing to all those You bring into my life. Amen.

PART THREE

Simply Smart Regarding Money

IF WE PLAN NOW, we will have ample opportunity to make wise decisions regarding our finances. I have filled these pages with resources from financial professionals who offer wisdom and practical suggestions on how to plan for the retirement of your dreams. You may need to change your attitude about how you spend money now but with God's help, you can find a plan that will work for you. So get out a pencil and paper and make notes on questions to ask and tasks to accomplish so that you will be "simply smart" when it comes to planning for future financial security.

Money, Your Gender and Your Personality

If anyone does not provide for his relatives,
and especially for his immediate family, he has
denied the faith and is worse than an unbeliever.

—1 TIMOTHY 5:8 (NIV)

When it comes to money, investing and saving for retirement, women often fall prey to what some might call "the gender gyp." "Women as a group tend to put others before themselves," says Emily Sanders, president of Sanders International, Inc., a financial-advisory firm in Norcross, Georgia. She says, "That's a good thing on one hand; it makes us compassionate and caring. But we shortchange ourselves in our financial well-being." Despite our gains in the workplace, when it comes to creating a secure retirement, we still face bigger obstacles than men. Our paychecks are still smaller, as are our pensions.

On average, women stay home 11.5 years to raise children, which takes them out of the workforce and reduces their future Social Security benefits. And married couples too often give short attention to building a wife's nest egg. They simply assume that the husband's retirement savings will be sufficient. But life brings surprises that can quickly change such expectations. A woman can suddenly find herself widowed or divorced.

Unexpected financial independence can be especially frightening and damaging if the wife has little or no knowledge about her family finances. The story of one such woman appeared in the *St. Louis Senior Circuit*. Mary was a devoted wife and mother of two sons. She and her husband John earned about $80,000 a year. They were comfortable and more than able to provide a nice life for themselves and their children. But all of this vanished suddenly when John was swept off the deck of his boat and thrown overboard in the middle of the Atlantic Ocean. They never found his body. After the initial shock wore off, another nightmare began. Mary had no clue where her husband kept their money. He had been in complete financial control. She was lost. It took her nearly a year to get help from a professional certified financial planner.

After my divorce, I too realized just how savvy I wasn't. I was much better off than Mary was, since I actually handled the monthly expenses. But my husband had handled all the investments. That was scary for me. Ms. Sanders says, "Every woman—regardless of which spouse handles money matters—should have a basic understanding of family finances and retirement planning. At the very least, women should know where the assets are. They should read tax returns before they sign them, and they should know where all the important documents are kept."

ACKNOWLEDGE YOUR SPENDING PERSONALITY

But it's not just our gender that affects our perspective on money. Our money "personality" also plays a big factor in how we manage financially. Olivia Mellan, a Washington, D.C., psychotherapist, author and money coach, sees it all the time. "Every one of us has personality blind spots when it comes to money." Our decisions about money are often driven by psychological factors over which we have little conscious control. As a result, we make mistakes that can negatively affect our long-term interests. Vincent Wood, president of AdvisorTeam.com, a behavioral research and testing firm in San Francisco, developed a *Money* magazine test. It is built upon a standard personality profiling system called the Kersey Temperament Sorter. Four categories were discovered: guardians, who tend to be cautious with their money; artisans, who are freewheeling and daring; idealists, who care less about money than other goals; and rationals, who make most decisions by the numbers."[9]

Of course, most of us are a mix of these different types. But still, we will have a strong affinity to one or at most two of the categories, according to the researchers. The guardians place greater importance on financial security than on getting rich. I seem to most resemble this type. We are disciplined and patient, and enjoy organizing and planning ahead. We would rather invest than spend and we investigate carefully before committing. We are the least likely to invest in a double-or-nothing proposition.

The idealist tends to focus on assisting others and improving society rather than on building personal wealth. I have a friend like this. Several months ago, we had a serious talk about money. She is a single mom and is always struggling financially, despite the fact that she has a master's degree and should be earning a decent wage. When I told her that money was not the root of all evil and that only the love of money was evil, she cried. I think all these years she somehow thought money was bad. The truth is, it's simply necessary. Idealists lack interest in money matters and that can lead them to fail in reaching their financial goals—assuming they even set any. Idealists must remember that they can do more for others if they are financially secure themselves.

Rationals are the "cool" ones. They enjoy problem solving and fact-finding, and they have a deep interest in science and the latest technology. They tend to stay calm when things get out of hand. But this cool attitude can make them a bit too sure of themselves. More than any other type they are inclined to put together their own financial plan and pick their own investments. The thing they don't seem to understand is that the stock market is not always rational. Simply thinking you can outsmart the market doesn't make it happen. Rationals are the group most willing to take a lot of risk with some of their money.

Artisans trust their gut. They are the entrepreneurial type or performer. They enjoy the thrill of investing. They act quickly and are comfortable taking risks. But . . . they tend to lack interest in the long-term planning and discipline needed to reach their goals. Artisans must guard against following every impulse. Statistics say that artisans more than any other type would jump at a double-or-nothing opportunity with fifty percent odds of success. The best course for an artisan is automatic investing.

Self-knowledge is the key to defending yourself against your weaknesses and taking advantage of your strengths. Behavioral finance expert Meir Statman says, "If you understand your temperament, you can better manage financial risk and plan your goals, and perhaps become more successful in other walks of life as well."

Educate yourself. Just because you find finances confusing or forbidding doesn't mean you should ignore them. Women face greater economic challenges in retirement simply because they live longer than men. According to the *St. Louis Circuit* at www.seniorcircuit.net, we amass thirty-four percent fewer pension dollars than men. We have a lot at stake. **START GAINING FINANCIAL SAVVY** by having a family meeting to find out what your financial story is—and where it's headed.

MAKE SURE YOUR SPOUSE HAS ALL THE FACTS. Even if you and your mate are fit as fiddles, be certain that you both know what to do if something should happen to either one of you. Streamline your investment accounts as much as possible. Make sense out of your filing system. Start by creating a folder for each separate account. Save brokerage and mutual fund statements, along with trade confirmations. Throw out annual reports, prospectuses and marketing literature. Make a master directory, listing all of your accounts and account numbers. Don't forget about any insurance policies either. Include the names and phone numbers of any individuals you deal with at various financial institutions along with passwords and the like. Store this information in a secure place, such as a safety deposit box, and tell your spouse where it is.

CLARIFY YOUR GOALS. "Too many retirement stories today are out there to scare you," says Jean Chatzky, financial editor of *Today* magazine. Instead of thinking just in numbers, focus on how you really want to live and how much that will cost. Be realistic. If you have always dreamed of traveling in retirement, then plan for it. You can't travel and maintain your current lifestyle on fifty percent less income. Others truly want a simpler life—fifty percent might just be the perfect number for them.

Lord, help me to see the truth about my present spending habits and my future needs. Give me wisdom today for preparing for tomorrow's needs so that, like the Proverbs woman, I can laugh at the days to come. Amen.

The Money Menu

With money in your pocket, you are wise and
you are handsome and you sing well too.

—YIDDISH PROVERB

Assuming this proverb to be true, then the opposite must also be true: With no money in your pocket, you are unwise, unattractive and you don't sing very well either. A poll conducted by Fidelity Investments bears this out, at least in part: More than half of retirees regret poor planning. While two-thirds of retirees are living the lifestyle they hoped for, more than half wish they had planned differently in their final working years. Two-thirds of those polled said they had not completed a budget for their retirement years, while three out of four did not have an asset allocation strategy to manage their income while retired. The song they are singing now may not be pretty, but it can be valuable to those of us who have not yet retired.

According to the survey, there are four basic lessons we can learn. Lesson One: Put the maximum in your company's 401(k) plan. If your company matches a part of what you save, recognize that this is free money. If I offered to double your money, would you refuse me? Of course not, yet every day, thousands of people neglect to participate in something so simple and valuable.

Lesson Two: Don't let your lifestyle outpace your income. Christine Fahlund, a senior financial planner with T. Rowe Price, says that one of the biggest obstacles to saving for retirement is our tendency to accelerate our lifestyle. In other words, rather than save more money as our income goes up, we spend it.

Lesson Three: Know how you will replace your paycheck. Sadly, most of us retire with no real plan for turning savings into income. The Fidelity survey mentioned above found that "even though many retirees regretted not having paid more attention to income, fifty-one percent said they still didn't know which assets to tap first." Many people simply don't understand the options they have, other than cashing out their savings and paying ordinary income taxes.

Lesson Four: Don't be too quick to leave work. According to Dallas Salisbury, president of Employee Benefit Research Institute, "If you have a job with a retirement plan and health insurance the employer pays at least part of and you're not miserable, the longer you stay the better off you are." And the more comfortable your retirement will be.

DEVELOP THREE PRIMARY RETIREMENT SOURCES

There should be three major elements to any retirement plan: savings and investments, pensions and your Social Security benefits. Unfortunately, there are many people (especially women) who only have one of the three elements in place, and that is Social Security. The reality is that Social

Security was never meant to be a retirement plan in itself. It was simply a safety net to keep us from financial devastation.

To make the most of your Social Security benefits, you must avoid early retirement. Full retirement age differs depending on when you were born. If you were born in 1941, you must be sixty-five and eight months of age to collect full benefits. If you were born in 1955, for example, you must be sixty-six and two months of age before retiring. I was born in 1951—that means I must be sixty-six before I can receive full Social Security benefits. If you choose to take early retirement and start collecting at age sixty-two, you could see as much as a twenty-five percent reduction in benefits. How much will you get? That depends on how much you or your spouse has earned.

Your Social Security benefit calculations are based on your average earnings during a lifetime of work. Most of us will receive the average of our thirty-five highest years of earnings. Years in which we have low earnings or no earnings may be counted to bring the total years of earnings up to thirty-five. If both you and your husband work, you will each get your own benefit. If you are widowed and your accumulated benefit is less than your husband's, then you would receive your own amount plus enough to bring the benefit amount up to be equal to half of your husband's. In other words, if your husband receives $1,450 a month, you would receive $725 a month. Even if you are divorced, you can collect Social Security benefits from your ex-husband's fund. As long as you were married for at least ten years and are currently not married, you will receive a monthly check from the U.S. government based on your ex-husband's Social Security record.

When it comes to taking care of ourselves in retirement, we women must get serious. We need to slash our overhead costs and start saving. The simplest way to save is to make it automatic. I have $400 taken out of my paycheck each month that goes directly into my 401(k). If I don't have it, I won't spend it. I try to keep things simple enough to manage myself. But I do have a wonderful investment counselor whom I trust implicitly. I am conservative and patient. I am also a realist. I plan on working, at least part-time, for as long as I can. Worry? Not me. It's a waste of time. As a friend of mine told me many years ago, "If worrying would put one penny in your pocket, I would tell you to worry. But it won't, so don't." I figure, like Carol Kuykendall found out, that there are better things I can do with my time than worry:

> "I can't do it!" I cried in frustration as I stood beside our horse trailer in a crowded parking lot at the county fairgrounds that hot July afternoon. When I arrived early that morning with my daughters Lindsay and Kendall and their two horses, I did what I always do at 4-H horse shows. I positioned the car and trailer widely across two lanes, assuring myself of a straight-ahead path to exit because in three years of hauling horses, I have never learned to back up our trailer. The plan always worked—until today. While I was in the arena watching the girls, the parking lot filled up and someone started a new row in front of me. Now I was boxed in with nothing to do but back out or hope the people in front of us would return before we wanted to leave. I felt helpless, so I prayed and put the problem in the Lord's hands.
>
> "You know I can't back up this horse trailer," I complained, "and I'm embarrassed to admit I need help. So please clear my path before we have to leave." Thinking I had done

all I could do, I started back into the arena where I worried my way through the afternoon.

When the girls finished their events, we returned to the parking lot to discover we were still boxed in. "I'll get Mrs. Greenlee," Lindsay said. "She's not afraid of backing trailers." I winced, but within a few minutes our problem was solved, thanks to perky Mrs. Greenlee.

Yet my embarrassment sparked some clear thinking as we drove home. God doesn't want us merely to put our problems in His hands. Sure, He wants our prayers but He also wants to use us in the answers to those prayers. He wants us to *do* something. That's Tandem Power. "I pray as if it depended upon God," Mother Teresa once said. "But I work as if it depended upon me." I thought of other nagging worries that I could do something about. I worry about finances because I don't know enough about budgeting. About entertaining because I haven't cultivated some no-fail "company" dinners. About driving alone in the big city because I don't know my way around.

How about you? Do you have a worry caused by something you can learn? Why don't you whittle away at that worry this month by taking a single step of action: Sign up for a class or polish a rusty skill. As for me, every time we hitch up our horse trailer this month, I vow to back it once around our circular driveway. With God's help.

Don't hesitate to **ASK FOR HELP**. Pray about from whom you should seek counsel. The Bible teaches in Proverbs 15:22 that plans fail from a lack of counsel. Interview at least three financial planners before you hire anyone. Meet each planner face-to-face to make sure you get along. Find out as much as you can about them and the services they provide. Check their credentials. A certified financial planner (CFP) must pass an examination, work for a certain number of years and agree to follow a code of ethics. Request and check out references. Be sure to talk to several people who have worked with the planner for at least three years. Ask what they would change about their relationship, if anything. Be sure to get a written summary of the money you would be paying in fees and commissions. Find out their specialty. They should have a working knowledge of taxes, insurance, estate planning, retirement planning, investing and family budgeting. Be sure the planner will act as your "fiduciary." A fiduciary owes the client the utmost care and loyalty. Get this in writing. The Financial Planning Association can be contacted at (800) 282-PLAN or visit their Web site at www.fpanet.org; Certified Financial Planners Board of Standards: (888) 237-6275, www.cfp.net; The National Association of Personal Financial Advisors: (888) FEE-ONLY, www.napfa.org; and the American Institute of Certified Public Accountants: www.aicpa.org.

Be smart about your pension. When you retire you usually have the option of taking a lump sum and rolling it over into an IRA, or to take an annuity that pays an annual stream of income. **WEIGH YOUR PAYOUT OPTIONS.** If you don't expect to buy many big-ticket items in retirement, an annuity may meet your needs by providing a steady paycheck every month. However, if you will need large sums of money from time to time, you may be better off taking a lump sum and rolling it over into an IRA. Pay attention to interest rates. As interest rates rise, a lump-sum benefit will take a hit and go down. An annuity is a good choice if your family has longevity because the longer you live, the more money you make on an annuity. But annuities don't offer much flexibility. If you are way up in years, an annuity does not make sense. An eighty-four-year-old grandmother has no need to accumulate—she simply needs income. Annuities have two phases: accumulation, which can last for years, and then distribution. It's absurd for older retirees to invest the bulk of their liquid assets in an instrument that locks away money for years.

MAXIMIZE WITHDRAWALS FROM YOUR IRA when you are in the lowest possible tax bracket. According to Frank Armstrong III, CFP, founder of Investor Solutions, Inc., "If you are nearing retirement age, your IRA is well into seven figures and your taxable income puts you into the twenty-five percent or lower federal bracket, it is probably smart to make withdrawals to benefit from the low bracket now. They might even spare you from future tax rates as high as thirty-five percent once minimum required distribution begins." Armstrong also suggests converting some or all of your traditional IRA to a Roth IRA instead of withdrawing money from your IRA. (A Roth IRA allows a person to set aside after-tax income up to a specified amount each year. Earnings on this account are tax free, and tax-free withdrawals may be made after age fifty-nine and a half.) Then you will never pay tax on withdrawals.

Educate yourself and the next generation of women. Start with the Social Security Administration's guide, "What Every Woman Should Know." It's available at the agency's site: www.ssa.gov. Also **HELP THE NEXT GENERATION BY ENCOURAGING YOUR DAUGHTER OR GRANDDAUGHTER TO JUMP-START HER RETIREMENT PLANS**. An annual contribution of $3,000 to a Roth IRA for just five years, commencing when a woman is seventeen years old (assuming she had earned income) and continuing until age twenty-two, could yield a nest egg of one million dollars when she reaches age sixty-five, thanks to the magic of tax-sheltered compounding.

Lord, just as You taught Joseph to save for coming years of famine, by faith I will save for my latter years. Help me to develop financial wisdom for investing the talents You have given me now for a return that honors You in my future. Amen.

Stretching Your Money

A rich man is nothing but a poor man with money.

—W. C. FIELDS, AMERICAN ACTOR
(1880–1946)

Just thinking about living on a fixed income can be scary. And sometimes a fixed income isn't fixed. Most of us have money invested in the stock market and other variable interest accounts. That means our income will go up and down depending on what the financial world is doing. As I am writing this, many experts are suggesting that we need once again to be on the alert for a recession. As we move toward retirement, we simply need to change how we think about money.

The need for a new perspective on money will be especially necessary if the last several years have been your highest earning years. It's always harder to step down in lifestyle. But ultimately, your goal is to make your money last as long as you do. That does not mean you must die with a fortune. In fact, I am going to do my best to make my money last just as long as I do.

Have you ever overpaid for something? Most of us have at one time or another. When it comes to retirement spending, we simply have to be more careful. We must become penny-pinchers. But, as Cecil Scaglione wrote in the *St. Louis Senior Circuit*, "Being a penny pincher does not mean you buy 'cheap.' It means you make certain you get what you want and good value for what you pay. It doesn't mean you buy the cheapest cut of steak. It means you buy the cut with the least fat and bone on it."

One of the first things to look at is taxes. At one time there were more tax breaks for seniors. But today, a number of cash-strapped state and local governments are cutting back on property tax breaks for the elderly, even as many seniors are struggling to pay the rising taxes on their homes as assessments have soared. My municipality reassessed last year. Many homes actually doubled in assessment value—making taxes fly through the roof. In addition to property taxes, there are state income taxes, sales taxes, excise taxes, license taxes, intangible taxes, and estate and inheritance taxes to be considered! It's clear that taxes are increasingly important to everyone, but especially to retirees.

Many people planning to retire use the presence or absence of a state income tax as the litmus test for choosing a retirement destination. But the lack of a state tax doesn't always ensure that you will have a low total tax burden. Jan Cullinane and Cathy Fitzgerald, authors of *The New Retirement*, did a lot of research on which states provide the best overall tax benefits for seniors. They researched studies by Kiplinger, Bloomberg and The Tax Foundation. In their final study there was no consensus: "There isn't one state that is found on all lists as being either tax friendly or tax unfriendly. The results of the studies all depend on the assumptions made when doing the analysis."[10] In the end, the one thing they were sure of is that each state needs to raise revenue in order to meet its obligations.

The tax rates and the various exemptions, such as for retirement income, vary by state and by type of tax. Your individual situation is what should be used to assess which state offers the most tax savings for you. Only by consulting with a certified public accountant, particularly one that specializes in individual taxation, can you truly make an intelligent decision. For example, one man wanted to sell his business in Kentucky and move to Florida for retirement. His tax adviser told him that by moving to Florida first, and establishing a domicile residency there, and *then* selling the stock in his business, he would avoid having to pay Kentucky income tax on the sales profit. That gave him a much larger retirement budget.

DIFFERENTIATE BETWEEN NEEDS AND WANTS

As I mentioned earlier in the book, our homes can help or hurt us financially in retirement. One of the first questions regarding your home that you should ask is whether or not you should have a mortgage. Many of us hope to have our homes paid off by retirement age. But sometimes having debt is actually financially rewarding. Cullinane and Fitzgerald also confirm AARP's recommendation saying, "You can justify having mortgage debt in retirement if, by borrowing, you invest the dollars not spent on the house, generating after-tax returns that exceed the after-tax costs of the mortgage (interest only)."[11] For example, if you borrow $100,000 with an interest rate of five percent, your cost of borrowing is $5,000 per year. Since the $5,000 interest is tax deductible on your income taxes, you pay only about $4,000 for borrowing $100,000. You then invest the $100,000 and earn more than the $4,000 it cost you to borrow it.

As we reach our golden years, we simply must learn to take advantage of all the discounts that are available. We must also change the way we think about money. As our paycheck goes away, our ability to track and monitor our spending must accelerate. In the end, it's about being aware of how and what we spend and maintaining an attitude that matches the reality of our financial picture. That's just what Guideposts writer Wally Metts did when he faced a new money reality:

> Recessions are funny things. We don't know how long or how bad they will be. Analysts worry because people will spend less at holidays like Christmas and not buy new cars every four years. All around, the economy looks bad.
>
> When these economic forecasts crop up in the news, it makes me wonder why I get so worried. So I won't buy a new car—the old one's been running fine and it's already scratched so I won't have those "new car worries." I'll spend less at Christmas—its focus has become far too commercial anyway. And I won't be able to afford a new, upgraded home—I'll have to be content with the plumbing, heating, repairing, furnishing and landscaping of this one.
>
> I can easily let gloomy forecasts scare me. But having come from the "outhouse generation," I know I've gotten along just fine with a lot less than I have now. I get discontented over the things I want, not over the things I have. The Lord knows the difference between genuine neediness and "wantiness." He's there to help the needy, but the "wanty" will have to learn to be content with what they have.

BE SHREWD. Purchase the least expensive home in a good neighborhood. That is what I have always done. These homes appreciate more quickly. Pay off debts. Start with the ones that have the highest interest rates, especially if they are not deductible, such as credit cards and auto loans. Be careful with credit cards. Pay attention to all updated information regarding minimum payment changes and interest rate updates. Remember also that little things add up. Carry only as much cash in your wallet as you can afford to spend. Do not carry your credit card unless you know you are going to need it for a particular situation. Lower your insurance premiums by taking higher deductibles for your car and homeowner's insurance. Check your life insurance policy rates from time to time. Evaluate whether you actually need life insurance at this stage of your life.

CONSIDER ALL YOUR HEALTH INSURANCE OPTIONS. A program called Medical Advantage from AARP is available in twenty-one states and covers those fifty to sixty-four. It includes physician visits, medical tests and surgery. To check out other health insurance options go to www.eHealthInsurance.com to compare plans. Choose the best Medicare health plan for you. You can call them at (800) MEDICARE. You can also go online at www.medicare.gov and click on "Medicare Personal Plan Finder" in the first column, lower left. You will be able to narrow down the plan that is best for you. Always review very, very carefully all hospital bills. One gal found out that she was charged $129 for a box of tissues. Also, don't forget to question any insurance denials for coverage. Recently, I found that my insurance provider was having computer trouble (for nearly six months ongoing) that was denying payment for services. The computer glitch said that I needed preapproval. The reality is that

I did not. I finally got the insurance provider to call the hospital and explain that it was a computer problem that was going to take at least six more weeks to resolve. The hospital agreed to wait and resubmit the invoices at a later date rather than continue to call me for payment.

USE OTHER RESOURCES. Check out www.cheapskatemonthly.com or www.stretcher.com for tips and ideas for saving money every day. Some of the ideas that Cheapskate Monthly recommends include looking high and low when grocery shopping. You will usually find the less expensive store or generic brands at the bottom and top of the shelves; the higher-priced name brands are "conveniently" located at eye level. Make, and stick with, a grocery list. When you find yourself picking up an item that is not on your list, place it in the child's seat of the shopping cart. Then just before checking out, reevaluate the budget-breaking items and make yourself put all of them back except for one item. Mary Hunt of Cheapskate Monthly also recommends that you avoid shopping on the first day or two of the month because some stores have been known to raise their prices during the time that welfare and Social Security checks are issued. For a wealth of great ideas, check out Mary Hunt's book *Tiptionary*.

Lord, please help me to become aware of the difference between needs and wants. I want to be a good steward of all You have entrusted to my use. Amen.

Avoiding the Big Rip-off

The thief cometh not, but for to steal,

and to kill, and to destroy. . . .

—JOHN 10:10 (KJV)

A person who takes the property of another is a thief. Although some thieves use violence, most use surprise to break in and steal. Perhaps that's why fraud and scams are the number one crime against seniors. Whether it's a vacuum cleaner salesman, a home repair contractor, time-shares, stocks and bonds, financial planning or a winning lottery ticket, seniors tend to be more trusting and less likely to suspect a con artist.

Elderly people are often lonely and susceptible to a friendly pitch. They are also more likely to be at home to answer the door or telephone. The U.S. Office of Consumer Affairs warns that, while everyone is fair game for these crooks, the elderly are especially vulnerable because they are home and many try to be polite. The victimization of senior citizens is a growing problem, but one that largely goes unnoticed because seniors are reluctant to report problems if and when they realize there is one. They often resist taking action against the perpetrator because they are embarrassed and afraid that it will jeopardize their autonomy if family members think they cannot take care of themselves.

Diane Gibbons, a deputy district attorney in San Diego who prosecutes crimes against seniors, says, "It's hard to determine how many seniors are victimized because they don't come forward. Sometimes the crimes involved family members. Often, the seniors are just too embarrassed to report the crime, fearing they'll lose their independence." Gibbons also advised, "You don't want to take away their dignity and treat them like they are two years old, but that doesn't mean you can't get involved in their financial situation."

Several factors make senior citizens top targets for financial abuse: isolation, loneliness and their willingness to trust others. Ann Flaherty, executive director of ElderAngels, confirms the findings of others, saying, "They're home all the time. Often, they're happy to get attention from a stranger who feigns interest in their well-being or tries to befriend them."

Sally Hurme who writes for AARP, says we need to beware of false "new friends." One eighty-three-year-old gentleman was befriended by a young couple and their children two years ago. His son just discovered that over the past year his dad has given them most of the money in his checking and savings accounts. All he has left is his house. This is a classic case of financial exploitation that often begins with a new friend who connives and further isolates a person from his own family, then slowly takes control of his finances.

One of the most common travel scams against the fifty-year-old-plus crowd is receiving a travel certificate in the mail notifying you by name that you've won a luxury vacation to some exotic island. Part of the reason we are targeted for this scam is that older Americans typically have more disposable income and travel a lot. You think you're getting a great deal. But you wind up paying more for the "bargain" than you anticipated. The airfare may be free, but wait until you see the bill for the hotel! CNN Money experts say, "These 'you've-won-a-trip' solicitations are deceptively worded and usually precede come-ons for lengthy spiels on time-share investments—something else experts suggest you steer clear of."

"BE WISE AS SERPENTS"

AARP reports that as more and more seniors get computer savvy, opening e-mail accounts, surfing the Internet and paying bills online, travel fraud has extended into cyberspace. You receive an e-mail congratulating you that you've won a trip. To claim the prize, winners are told to call a phone number and give their credit card information. The mere fact that e-mail is cheap makes it easier for criminals to thrive via the Internet.

Phony lotteries and other sweepstakes are repeatedly run by scam artists who are extremely persistent and persuasive. Elder Options of Texas received a call from a senior consumer who wanted to verify that a sweepstakes was legitimate. She had been notified that she had won a sweepstakes and had been instructed to wire money to Costa Rica to pay for the so-called franchise tax. A person who claimed to be from the Florida Customs Office contacted her directly and assured her that the sweepstakes was legitimate.

Greg Abbott, Attorney General of Texas, said, "Whenever you are asked to pay any money, for any reason, in order to claim a prize, you are dealing with a crook. The requirement to wire money, rather than using U.S. mail, is another tip-off. Do not accept verification from someone who calls. Anyone can call you and say anything!"

Predatory lenders also target seniors. The practice occurs when some lenders pressure homeowners into high-interest loans they may not be able to repay. Predatory loans are often packed with excessive fees, costly credit insurance and balloon payments. A friend of mine fell victim to this one. We have spent the last two years trying to get this monster refinanced but no one will touch it. She was going through some difficult financial times and was simply too embarrassed to ask for help. When she received the solicitation it seemed like the miracle cure to her financial worries. Dawn Sweeney, president of AARP Services, Inc., said, "Many homeowners are then stunned to find out that they cannot afford to pay off those loans and they may lose their homes."

Most of us know that there are scam artists out there when it comes to home repairs. Yet every day, someone gets swindled nonetheless. My mom is very savvy and as a kitchen and bath designer, she knows a lot more than the average person when it comes to hiring a contractor. Just the same, a few years ago, Mom hired a small contractor to replace her windows. She asked for and checked references. Fortunately, she only gave him a small deposit because he never showed.

The most notorious scammers in home-repair fraud are those that cruise neighborhoods and sell their services at your front door. Tom Kraeutler, a home inspector in New Jersey who hosts a nationally syndicated radio home-fix-it program called *The Money Pit*, says, "A promise to extend the life of asphalt or wood shingles with a recoating is a $1,000 rip-off that involves nothing but covering shingles with regular paint to make them look shiny and new." He also warns, "Don't fall for door-to-door driveway resealers who offer a bargain price to use the leftover materials from the last job. Chances are, your driveway may be recoated, for several hundred dollars, with used and useless motor oil."

DEVELOP A HEALTHY PARANOIA. Be suspicious of any unsolicited calls. Avoid business about which you know nothing. If you wish to pursue any such "good deals," get all the information you can about the company and verify it. Then take all this information to someone you trust and get his or her opinion. Don't be pressured. If something is that time-sensitive, it's not real. Beware of testimonials and check out financial planners thoroughly. Always check with The Better Business Bureau. Each state has its own agency overseeing stock and bond brokers. Many states have fraud divisions. The Nation Consumers League operates a Nation Fraud Information Center hotline with information referral services and assistance in filing complaints. The toll-free number is (800) 876-7060.

DEMAND A WRITTEN CONTRACT CLEARLY STATING WORK TO BE DONE before you pay a deposit for any home repair work. Never sign a home repair contract on the spot. Take time to read the contract thoroughly and have someone you trust also read it over. Never pay up front. Always obtain quotes from several companies and check references before you sign a contract. The contract should outline the work to be done, price, materials required and specific delivery and completion dates.

ASK YOURSELF A COUPLE OF CRUCIAL QUESTIONS. Before buying *anything* at your door, always ask yourself if you really need and want the product, if you can afford it, and whether the price is right. It's always a good idea to invite a friend or neighbor in when you hear a sales presentation from a door-to-door seller. If you want a salesperson to leave your home and they refuse, tell them you are calling the police to have them removed, and do it!

REPORT YOUR CONCERNS when you think someone is a bit too friendly. Whether it's you yourself that has been taken advantage of, or you suspect a friend or neighbor is being taken advantage of, call the authorities. You can report your concerns anonymously, if you wish. The hotline of adult protective services, the local agencies that are responsible for investigating suspected financial exploitation can be found online at www.elderabusecenter.org. Investigators are trained to distinguish between cases of genuine friendship and exploitations. If wrongdoing is suspected, they will turn over the case to law-enforcement authorities.

Don't let your pride get in the way. Call a friend, family member or the police. **IF YOU OR SOMEONE YOU KNOW IS THE VICTIM OF A FINANCIAL CRIME, THERE ARE STEPS YOU CAN TAKE** to recover your money or at the very least alert authorities to the activities of a serial swindler. Many police departments and district attorney's offices are creating elder abuse units. You might also contact your county's adult protective services agency. If you are taken in by an investment scam, call your state securities regulator. You might also contact the National Association of Securities Dealers at (800) 334-0668.

TAKE PREVENTIVE MEASURES. Don't give money to strangers who call or knock on your door. Simply hang up or shut the door. Be careful on the Internet. If you receive an e-mail advising that there is a problem with your bank account and requesting that you verify your account numbers, do not respond. Banks and other legitimate companies would not request personal information in this manner. Sometimes these e-mails direct you to bogus look-alike sites where identity thieves capture log-in names, passwords, account numbers and other data. Also, be careful not to inadvertently make a one-letter typo when typing in a popular Web address. Be careful of phony charities. If you receive a call from someone soliciting money for what sounds like a legitimate charity and a good cause, tell the caller that you need to think about it. You can always phone The Better Business Bureau to make sure the charity is legit. Contact The Better Business Bureau also to obtain a free tip booklet titled *Scams Against Seniors*.

Lord, please protect me from thieves and phony investments. Govern me with Your peace, and withdraw my peace whenever I am in danger so I will know to turn away to safety. Lead me clearly in the way I should go. Amen.

What to Leave Your Children?

People who want to get rich fall into temptation
and a trap and into many foolish and harmful desires
that plunge men into ruin and destruction.
For the love of money is a root of all kinds of evil. . . .

—1 TIMOTHY 6:9–10 (NIV)

A love of money distorts relationships with God and others. We must be sensitive to this and understand just how money can affect all relationships, but particularly how leaving wealth to our children will affect them and our relationship with them as well. Ron Blue wrote an article for the online magazine *thegoodsteward.com*, in which he said, "Leaving all your assets to your children must be preceded by 'a healthy portion of wisdom.' Deciding how generous you want to be goes beyond charitable giving. Just as you can give money to charity wisely or unwisely, you have strategic decisions to make when you think about passing on wealth to your kids."

Blue also says that no asset should be passed on without first giving your children "a healthy portion of wisdom." We all know that the best way to impart wisdom to children is to let them learn responsibility by having responsibility. Too often, parents who can afford it limit their children's experiences in managing money by doing it for them. When their children make a financial mistake, Mom and Dad run to the rescue.

I guess one of the questions that we should ask is "Are we obligated to leave money to our children?" I think the answer should be "It depends." As I wrote in *Managing Your Money* (an earlier book in this series), I have always struggled personally with handing money over to someone who has not earned it. My first question is "Whose money is it?" Obviously, it belongs to God. Does that obligate us to hand it over to the next generation? I think we must at least explore how God would have us use the money with which He has blessed us.

According to statistics from a Charles Schwab and Company wealth transfer survey, half of all Americans say that parents should strive to leave an inheritance to their children or beneficiaries: fifty-four percent say kids are entitled to an inheritance when a family has some level of wealth; forty-four percent expect to leave something to charity. Frankly, I don't think any child should expect parents who have little money to struggle or do without just so they can leave something behind. My feeling is that if you didn't earn it, you have no claim on it. I also think that it is misguided to live your life expecting to get rich some day simply because your parents died.

Besides, we must at least consider life-expectancy statistics that say we will live about thirty years in retirement. Frankly, most of those who are baby boomers are not going to be able to generate enough income with a conventional portfolio. Like it or not, they will most likely be dipping into their nest egg to survive thirty more years of living.

BE SURE TO LEAVE A LEGACY

Ultimately, we must consider what we really want to leave—a legacy or an inheritance. What's the difference? An inheritance usually refers only to financial wealth. Larry Burkett and Ron Blue, coauthors of *Wealth to Last*, says that a legacy "encompasses the intangibles as well—wisdom, character, reputation, and memories. It includes what can be added on a calculator and the words said at your funeral." He also says that our perspective on estate planning must be based on realities. For each of us, those realities differ. Some may have children with disabilities that preclude them from caring for themselves financially. But don't simply assume that a child with a disability needs or should be left more money. One family found after discussing this with a handicapped child that the child actually resented such an attitude.

None of us knows the future. None of us knows when we will die or the exact circumstances, financial or otherwise, that we may encounter along the way. Blue and Burkett believe that "good stewardship includes providing an inheritance for your family and being sure that every family member knows how to manage it. These decisions are not easy. Ask God to lead you in your decision."

Benjamin Franklin said, "Money never made a man happy yet, nor will it. There is nothing in its nature to produce happiness. The more a man has, the more he wants. Instead of filling a vacuum, it makes one. If it satisfies one want, it doubles and trebles that want another way. That was a true proverb of the wise man, rely upon it: 'Better is little with the fear of the Lord, than great treasure, and trouble therewith.'" Happiness and an appreciation for the sweetness of life is what a friend of Guideposts writer Brock Kidd inherited from his father:

"Life is sweet," my friend Allen Carter was saying. We were sitting in my room at the Sigma Chi House at the University of Tennessee. A few hours earlier, Allen had scored the points necessary to lead our intramural basketball team to victory. Naturally, I thought he was talking about winning the game. But I was wrong.

"I wish you could have known my dad, Brock," Allen said. I remembered that Allen's father had died when he was fourteen, and at first I felt a little uncomfortable as he talked on.

His father had been a successful lawyer, enjoyed farming, loved life. One day, as he watched Allen playing tennis, he began to feel dizzy, but he got an "all's clear" response from the doctor. Yet, a few months before his forty-ninth birthday on June 26, 1987, he was taken to surgery and a tumor in the speech area of his brain was diagnosed. On December 22 of that same year, at 6:30 in the morning, Allen's mom woke him, saying, "You'd better come. You'd better say good-bye to your father."

"I went in and said, 'I love you, Dad. I'm going to be with you again, someday,'" Allen remembered. "He grabbed my hand before he died."

I looked at my friend sitting across from me. His eyes were clear and there wasn't a glimmer of self-pity. To bridge the silence, I asked him what he felt was the most important thing his father left.

"He taught me," said Allen, "that life is sweet. And so I try to live my life that way. Maybe he's not here, but I know he's watching. I want him to see that I remember him by living as he lived."

Thinking back on that conversation, I see a lot of truth in Allen's words, and I can't help but recall the message of Jesus. When we believe, when we truly believe the things He taught us, we know that everything really is all right and that we will be together again with those we love. Suddenly, everything's okay. Suddenly, yes, as Allen said, "life is sweet." Very sweet.

SIMPLICITY MADE SIMPLE

Get a new perspective. A child does not have an automatic right to an inheritance. Looking at it from a legal perspective, state laws are very clear that **YOUR RESPONSIBILITY IS FIRST TO YOURSELF AND YOUR SPOUSE**, not to your adult children. Patricia Schiff Estess, author of *Money Advice for Your Successful Remarriage*, says, "One of the unstated social policies behind such laws is that the primary obligation of any married couple is to their own health and welfare first, their grown children's second."

KNOW YOUR MOTIVES. Linda Perlin Alperstein, an associate clinical professor at the University of California, says, "The question that parents have to ask themselves when considering a child's inheritance is, 'What do we want the money to say?'" She writes, "It's important to be aware of what's motivating you. There's a big difference between trying to preserve inherited money for a twenty-five-year-old who's not ready to handle it and trying to control that child. If, for example, you're worried about a child coming into a large sum when he or she is a novice at managing money, you might stagger the amounts so that the child will not get it all at once. That would be prudent. But if you directed the money not be paid out until "the child" reaches age sixty, that would be controlling—if not cruel."

DON'T CREATE OR EXACERBATE CONFLICTS among your children. Discussing your plans with your children will at least give you time to try to iron out any conflicts. Gerald Condon, coauthor of *Beyond the Grave* and a partner in the law firm Condon, Condon and Festa in Santa Monica, California, says, "Bringing the issue out into the open gives your kids venting time and allows you the opportunity to gauge their reactions. I've seen parents reconsider their actions after talking to children about their plans."

GIVE AWAY WHILE YOU ARE ALIVE, if you can afford to. That way, if one child needs more financial help or is more deserving, it may be better to provide the assistance while you're alive rather than to leave disproportionate sums in your will. Elyse Bencivenga and her husband of Brooklyn, New York, decided to focus on helping their children launch their careers now so they can become totally self-sufficient later. "They don't expect handouts, but they know if there's a money problem they can come to us, and we'll do what we can. And that's good. I want them to know that families share their resources and help each other out."

Lord, please show me where to plant the inheritance You have abundantly given me to invest. I want to be a good steward, and to put the wealth of both my heart and my finances in a place where it will continue to grow. Amen.

PART FOUR

Simply Prepared for a Happy Life

ONE OF THE GREATEST RESPONSIBILITIES we now face is to take advantage of the new technologies that help us remain healthy and active in a longer life span. Preventative health care is better than treatment, and there are many simple ways illustrated in this part of the book to ensure good health during the golden years. It's never too late for us to start some kind of exercise and proactive health plan. I will share many resources regarding health care and prescription plans and encourage you to get to know the effects of prescription drugs and over-the-counter medicines. After all, we share a common goal as long as we remain on earth—that is, to live happily ever after.

Promoting a Healthy Lifestyle

> Look to your health; and if you have it, praise God,
> and value it next to a good conscience; for health is
> the second blessing that we mortals are capable of;
> a blessing that money cannot buy.
>
> —IZAAK WALTON, ENGLISH WRITER
> (1593—1683)

I'm beginning to feel like an automobile. The older I get, the more maintenance I need. My assistant Patty said I should change my attitude and think of myself as a sexy red sports car instead of an old, beat-up sedan. That might be easier if I didn't develop a new ache or pain every time I turn around! Great improvements in medicine, public health, science and technology enable us to live longer and healthier than previous generations, but it also puts more responsibility for our health on us as individuals. Just because the science or technology is there, it does not make us instantly healthier. We still must do the work necessary to maintain our bodies.

Studies by the National Institute on Aging indicate that healthy eating, physical activity, mental stimulation, not smoking, active social engagement, moderate use of alcohol, maintaining a safe environment, social support and regular health care are important in sustaining health and independence. Did you notice that all nine of these suggestions require your taking responsibility for them to happen? Your health is in your own hands. Yet, all of us know someone who does more complaining than maintaining when it comes to health issues. Osteoporosis, breast cancer, high blood pressure, diabetes, heart disease, weight and obesity, and oral health, are just some of the areas that can be affected positively by learning more about disease prevention and health-promoting activities that will help us face, delay or manage these issues better.

Did you know that nine out of ten adults over the age of sixty-five go without appropriate health care screenings? Screening tests can catch conditions or diseases in their early stages, when they are treated more easily, and can also reduce substantially the impact of such illnesses as heart disease, hypertension, cancer and diabetes. In fact, many of these health conditions can be managed with simple lifestyle changes. A recent report from the Institute for Clinical Systems Improvement recommended that adults age sixty-five and older obtain preventive services every one to two years.

MedicineNet.com actually has a list of screenings that are beneficial in preventing diseases in women. Osteoporosis screening is one that I recently had done. I found out that I have osteoporosis in my hips and my femurs (upper leg bones). I'm petite and my mom has osteoporosis, so I wasn't completely surprised. But I was surprised at finding it in my legs. The DEXA bone scan is a critical screening process that can help you detect osteoporosis *before* fractures occur. It can also help predict the risk of future bone fractures. Knowing that we lose the most bone mass in the first five years after menopause puts me on the alert because I am only two years post-menopausal. As a result of this information, I had metabolic testing done to determine if I can metabolize calcium. Simply taking megadoses of calcium, when you cannot metabolize it, would only put your kidneys at risk. The metabolic testing indeed showed that I do not metabolize calcium. I am now on a diet to help normalize my system so that eventually I will be able to take calcium supplements to aid my osteoporosis.

The other screenings recommended for women by MedicineNet.com are breast cancer self-examination and mammography; blood pressure measurements; cancer of the cervix (PAP test); cancer of the colon and rectum/polyps of colon and rectum; elevated LDL cholesterol or low HDL cholesterol and triglycerides; melanoma—total body skin examination; diabetes and bladder cancer as well as glaucoma testing.

WATCH YOUR STEP

Diseases are not the only thing we should be looking to prevent or catch early. Falls are the biggest health risk for seniors today, according to the Web site Retirement with a Purpose (www.retirementwithapurpose.com). Falling down only takes a second, but recovering from a fall may take years and you may never be the same again. But falls do not have to be a normal part of aging. You can make simple changes to your living environment and your behavior that will help reduce your risk. Loose carpets, electrical and telephone cords, poor lighting, clutter, showers or tubs without grab bars and toilets without grab bars are all hazards that can easily be remedied. Pets and stairs can be a very big hazard when it comes to falls. One of my clients had a fatal fall when she tripped over her cat going down the basement stairs. As we age, we must train our loving pets to stay out of the way.

Ultimately, we cannot predict our health, but we can make a difference in it by caring for our bodies the way God expects us to. And that is exactly what Guideposts writer Mary Jane Clark discovered:

> In these months since my surgery and radiation treatments for cancer, my husband Harry and I have been learning all we can to make our lifestyle even healthier. We thought we were pretty good before (some of my family refer to me as the Earth Muffin), but now we're motivated to try even harder. As we explore some of the alternative approaches to health and wellness, we're finding a whole spectrum of ideas, from seriously weird to very reasonable. We're going for balance and moderation: Get some regular exercise; eat good, real food (more fruits and veggies, some soy, whole grains); and reduce stress.
>
> Even the mainstream medical community is increasingly recognizing the healing connection between our bodies and our minds. On one visit to our local hospital's Wellness Center, we were given two loaner tapes of exercises to aid in relaxation, stress reduction and strengthening the immune system.
>
> The day I went back to purchase one tape and return the other, I was helped by a pleasant young woman named Janet. She asked how I liked them.
>
> "I found them helpful," I replied, "but I confess I'm always a bit reserved about things like this unless I know more about the person who did them."

> With a smile she said, "I made the tapes."
>
> A bit hesitantly I asked, "Well, would you mind if I ask where you're coming from spiritually?"
>
> She paused for only a second and then said, "I'm a follower of Jesus Christ." No ambiguity, no defensiveness, just a clear and simple statement of her commitment.
>
> I bought both tapes. And I took something else with me that day as well: a reminder that I am called to live and speak in this world as a follower of Christ, with love and boldness.

Mary Jane Clark's story reminded me of a time when I was still a smoker. Someone said to me, "You cannot be a Christian if you smoke." I did not agree with the statement, but I had to admit that my faith did have something to say about smoking. If as a Christian I defile and abuse my body, which I believe to be the temple of the Holy Spirit, I am not a very good steward.

SIMPLICITY MADE SIMPLE

Don't set yourself up for a fall. According to the Web site Retirement with a Purpose, thirty-three percent of people age sixty-five and over will fall once a year. As I suggested above, **MAKE THE CHANGES IN YOUR ENVIRONMENT TO PREVENT A FALL**. Also, have your health care provider review your medications every six months to prevent multiple medications from causing dizziness, drowsiness and balance problems. Don't rush to answer a ringing phone. Many falls occur at about the fourth ring. Either purchase a cordless phone that you can hook to your waist or invest in an answering machine and check your messages at your convenience. Before jumping out of bed in the morning, sit on the edge of the bed and make sure you are not dizzy before you stand up. Also, bending over to reach low objects can cause lack of balance. Buy a long-handled "reacher" at a medical supply store for high-level item grabbing. Always eat breakfast. Skipping a meal could make you dizzy. And low blood pressure causes blackouts. Dizziness can also occur with hearing loss. Also, be sure your glasses have the right prescription for your current condition. If you can't see an object, you will trip over it.

SET UP REGULAR SCREENINGS. The Administration on Aging recommends having a risk management assessment every one to two years to review medications, height and weight, and blood pressure. Total cholesterol should be checked every five years. Mammograms are recommended to be done annually up until age seventy-five. The American Cancer Society recommends a skin check annually if you are over age forty. And don't forget to consider a flu shot; it is one of the best ways to fight the flu and to stay healthy. Remember, you should always be in communication with your doctor on any of these important medical precautions.

JOIN A GYM OR A LOCAL HEALTH PROGRAM. Seniors who stay active, are connected and have a health-supportive life experience are most likely to live longer and more independently. Unfortunately, thirty-five percent of those age sixty-five to seventy-four or older report not having time for any physical activity. If that's true, what are they doing with their time? Most seniors (eighty percent) have at least one chronic health condition, and fifty percent have at least two. Research has shown that seniors who have healthy lifestyles that include regular physical activity reduce their risk for chronic diseases and have half the rate of disability of those who do not.

Lord, I am thankful for the mobility that I still have. Each day that I am graced with limbs that move, I will strengthen them and remain ready for Your use. Amen.

The Prudent Use of Pharmaceuticals

Isaiah had said, "Prepare a poultice of figs and apply it to the boil, and he will recover."

—ISAIAH 38:21 (NIV)

The Bible only refers to medicines a few times. When childless Rachel begged Leah for some of her son's mandrakes, she was following an Eastern folk medicine tradition that supposedly promoted fertility. Isaiah 1:6 and Luke 10:34 both mention ointments and healing balms used to treat wounds. Here Isaiah was instructing that a poultice of figs be applied to King Hezekiah's boil. Gall and myrrh were often mixed with wine to be used as an anesthetic. And Paul encouraged Timothy to take a little wine for his chronic stomach problems.

Today some experts are predicting that by the year 2100, with the help of new medicines, the over-one-hundred crowd is expected to exceed five million! As pharmaceutical companies promise to continue to help us live longer and better, the real question is, "How can we afford to pay for these wonder drugs?" It seems the more medicine that is available, the more expensive the prescriptions become. Just yesterday I paid thirty dollars for twenty pills. And I have prescription medical coverage! They would have cost me forty-nine dollars otherwise. In 2002, the average American (some with drug coverage, some without) spent $487 on prescription drugs. However, adults age seventy-five and older spent about $1,028 annually.

The new Medicare drug benefit passed by Congress that is to start in 2006 is supposed to help seniors with the increasing costs of prescription medicine. The first thing to recognize about this new program is that it is very complicated. At least two plans will be available to everyone, with many more in some areas. Plans may charge different premiums and copays, as long as the overall value is at least as good as the standard package defined by Congress. Also, under the law the premiums may rise annually, depending on the amount.

And there are a few traps that you will need to take caution to avoid. If you do not sign up when you are first eligible for benefits, either in 2006, if you are already on Medicare, or when you turn age sixty-five, you must pay at least one percent more in premiums every month. In 2006, the monthly premium is expected to go up about thirty-five dollars per person. So if you are a healthy sixty-five-year-old in 2006, and you decide to wait four years before signing up, you will pay an extra forty-eight percent per month in premiums.

In addition to monthly premiums, there is a $250 annual deductible. After paying out that first $250, you must copay twenty-five percent of your drug costs up to $2,250 (minus the $250 deductible). But wait—this is where it gets really tricky—in order to save the government a bunch of money, there's a loophole: Congress created a "doughnut hole," meaning you must pay up to the required $2,250 out of your own pocket until you reach the next level, which is $5,100 in overall prescription drug costs. Then Uncle Sam will start paying again, but you still have to copay two dollars for every generic prescription and five dollars for brand-name drugs (or five percent, whichever is greater).

Now here's the other trap: All of these numbers can, and most likely will, change each year. For example, Charles Inlander, a health care consultant and president of the nonprofit Peoples Medical Society, says, "It's estimated that by 2008 the deductible will be $300 a year, and you will need to amass more than $6,000 in annual costs before the high-end of the program kicks in again." Ultimately, if you have $6,000 in annual drug costs, your out-of-pocket expenses, including copays, will be $4,065. In other words, you will save $1,935 a year by signing onto the new Medicare Drug Program. It's not great, but at least it is something, especially when you consider the predictions that by 2025, low-income females in poor health are expected to spend as much as $9,378 per year in out-of-pocket costs.

KNOW THE RISKS INVOLVED IN OTCs

As prescription prices rise, many of us are looking to over-the-counter drugs (OTCs) for cheaper alternatives. And that's a good thing, as long as you understand the dangers therein. Just because a medication is available without a doctor's prescription, that doesn't mean it's risk-free. Did you know, for example, that the leading cause of acute liver failure is a result of an overdose of acetaminophen, the active ingredient in Tylenol? Nonsteroidal, anti-inflammatories (NSAIDs) such as ibuprofen, which is in Advil, Excedrin IB, Midol Cramp, Motrin and Nuprin, as well as naproxen, the active ingredient in Aleve, are used to relieve pain, tenderness, inflammation and stiffness.

The danger is that they can cause gastrointestinal irritation and bleeding, peptic ulcers and kidney complications. They can also reduce the effectiveness of prescription ACE inhibitors and other blood-pressure-lowering medications. They can also cause rebound headaches. In other words, the pain reliever itself can cause headaches as the medicine builds up in the body.

Simple aspirin such as Bayer, Excedrin Extra Strength and St. Joseph's Adult Chewable Aspirin can cause stomach upset, vomiting, ulcers and inhibited blood clotting. For a while, I was having trouble with my gums bleeding. After I consulted with my dentist, I discovered that it was a result of my daily aspirin. It is also recommended that you consult with your doctor if you are taking steroids, such as hydrocortisone or prednisone or medication for gout or high blood pressure because they can all interact negatively with aspirin.

Acetaminophens such as Tylenol, Excedrin QuickTabs and Sudafed NonDrowsy Sinus Headache may cause liver damage if taken to excess, as I alluded to earlier. Calcium carbonate, which is used to relieve heartburn, acid indigestion and other stomach-related problems, may decrease the effectiveness of certain prescription medicines including the heart drug digoxin and the antibiotic tetracycline. You should not take calcium carbonate within two hours of taking any other medication.

Antihistamines such as Benadryl, Excedrin PM, Sominex, Tylenol PM and Unisom all have diphenhydramine, which can cause drowsiness and decreased mental alertness as well as memory loss. The decongestant pseudoephedrine, which is found in Sinutab, Sudafed, Advil Cold and Sinus and Tylenol Sinus Daytime, can cause increased blood pressure, rapid heartbeat and insomnia. I found this out the hard way when I took Sudafed for a stuffy nose so I could sleep—and then was wide awake for the entire night.

Cough syrup is another OTC that can have side effects you may not expect. Dextromethorphan, the antitussive that relieves a dry cough, is found in Benylin Cough Suppressant, Robitussin DM Cough Syrup, and Sucrets Eight-Hour Cough Suppressant, as well as Vicks Formula 44 Cough Relief. All can cause dizziness—and even hallucinations and seizures—if taken in excess.

Recently, a friend's seventeen-year-old son took several allergy and cough medicines over a period of four days. He ended up with a rash all over his body that required medical treatment by a physician. All of the drugs he took were OTCs, proving the point that just because you can buy it without a prescription doesn't mean it is safe. The more drugs we take, the smarter and more precautious we must become to avoid skyrocketing prices and keep ourselves safe.

SIMPLICITY MADE SIMPLE

Check out the **RESOURCES FOR MORE INFORMATION ON NONPRESCRIPTION PRODUCTS** online at www.fda.gov. Click on "Drug Information," then "Over-the-Counter Drug Information" or call (301) 827-2222. For a chart of drugs containing acetaminophen or NSAIDs, go to www.familydoctor.org.

START TALLYING YOUR PRESCRIPTION DRUG COSTS NOW to be ready for the Medicare Drug Program. AARP's Web site at www.aarp.org has a drug benefit calculator to help you figure out if you will actually realize a savings. Most Medicare beneficiaries are expected to save money by joining. If the drug plan doesn't make economic sense for you, look into discount prescription cards, which are available from your pharmacy or drug company. Some of the drug companies offering discount cards are Eli Lilly, Merck, Glaxo-SmithKline, Novartis, Pfizer and Bristol-Myers.

PRICE SHOP. Prescription drug prices can vary by twenty-five percent or more from one pharmacy to another. Price shop by phone. Marv Shepherd, PhD, director of the Center for Pharmacoeconomic Studies, suggests calling in the evening or weekday afternoons when pharmacists are typically less busy. Buy online. This is what I do. You can save anywhere from twenty percent to fifty percent buying drugs from an online provider. I've used Medco, www.medco.com. Another reputable online pharmacy is Express Scripts, www.expressscripts.com. Be sure to only buy from online pharmacies that display the Verified Internet Pharmacy Provider Site (VIPPS) seal. This means that they have been inspected and accredited by the National Association of the Boards of Pharmacy. If you have your doctor write your prescription for three months worth of medicine, you will save the most.

Request older drugs. I don't mean out-of-date old, but older versus new types of drugs. Even doctors can be influenced by the slick marketing campaigns of the major drug companies. And the newer drugs are often far more expensive. Ask your doctor to write prescriptions for older, less expensive drugs unless there is a compelling medical reason not to. **USE GENERIC DRUGS.** Sadly, many of us think that generic means less quality. But generic drugs are equivalent to brand-name drugs. Before a generic can be sold, the U.S. Food and Drug Administration makes sure the drug is just as effective as its patented brand-name version. Generics can really save you money. The average price of a brand-name prescription in 2002 was $76.29, compared with $22.79 for a generic. To find out if a generic is available, go to the FDA's Web site at www.fda.gov for a list of all FDA-approved drugs and generic equivalents.

Father, I am grateful for all the healing agents You have given us in order to live a longer and healthier life. Give me wisdom on when to take medicine and when to simply take a nap. Amen.

Diet, Exercise and Your Mind

"So I have come down to rescue them from the hand
of the Egyptians and to bring them up out
of that land into a good and spacious land,
a land flowing with milk and honey. . . ."

—EXODUS 3:8 (NIV)

Israel's varied topography made it possible to cultivate a great variety of foods. The Bible mentions figs, apples, pomegranates, grapes, olives, pistachios and almonds. Olives were pressed to produce a light and tasty cooking oil. Milk products provided essential protein in the Hebrew diet. Seven ritually clean wild animals are also mentioned. Both ocean and freshwater fish, caught in the Sea of Galilee, were important foods. Honey provided a delightful element to their diet. God truly gave his people a land rich in agricultural resources. It was a productive land that "flowed with milk and honey." As long as God's people lived in harmony with the Lord, they enjoyed the land's bounty and had all they needed for a healthy and prosperous life.

September 26, 2005, was fitness guru Jack LaLanne's, ninety-first birthday. I have watched him on television, when he was selling his juicer. He looks amazing and is healthier than most sixty-year-olds. In an interview for *USA Today*, he said, "You've got to work at living—99.9 percent of Americans work at dying! You've got to eat right, exercise and have goals and challenges. Exercise is king; nutrition is queen. Put 'em together and you've got a kingdom!" What's remarkable is how far ahead of his time LaLanne really was. Now, all the doctors and fitness experts agree that physical exercise is critically important for brain health, because it gets oxygen, sugar (as glucose) and nutrients to the brain. In addition, older people who stay active in a wide variety of ways seem to have a better chance of warding off dementia.

Dr. Constantine Lyketsos, a Johns Hopkins University epidemiologist and the lead author of a new study, says, "It's the variety that matters." Researchers tracked 3,375 men and women over the age of sixty-five from 1992 to 2000, surveying them on the kinds of activities they did. What they found is that those doing the widest variety of exercises were far less likely to develop dementia. And that is what LaLanne has been saying since 1951. LaLanne advises, "You have to take care of your 640 muscles, and the number one thing is exercise. You can eat perfectly but if you don't exercise, you cannot get by." He says, "So many older people, they just sit around all day long and they don't get any exercise. Their muscles atrophy, and they lose their strength, their energy and vitality by inactivity." LaLanne believes that your body is your mind's servant. It's simply a matter of your brain telling your body to get moving.

At the California Senior Games in San Diego, most of the competitors, ranging in age from fifty to ninety-plus, agree that living younger longer starts in the head. By refusing to believe that the pace of aging is fixed, they've "exercised" their right to feel young. Dr. Mike Magee, senior medical adviser for Pfizer, a sponsor of the National Senior Games Association, said, "The reality of it is they have about the same percentage of chronic disease as the general public. The difference is that they've seen a doctor early enough to prevent organ damage and control their disease rather than let it control them." Dr. Alex Leif of the Harvard Medical School of Gerontology says, "Ultimately, though, most have found that the best medicine is exercise. It's the closest thing to an antiaging pill there is."

Besides exercise, LaLanne also believes in eating right. He is primarily a vegetarian who only eats fish—no chicken, no turkey, just fish. He drinks six or seven glasses of water a day. And he has at least five or six pieces of fresh fruit every day and ten raw vegetables.

Sadly, if you're over fifty, you're probably not eating right, according to Helen Rasmussen, RD, Tufts University. She says, "Research shows that as people age, they consume fewer calories. Older adults are less active and their metabolism has slowed, which decreases appetite." The other reason they tend to eat less is that those who live alone often eat small, irregular meals, which may not contain nutritious food choices.

IDLENESS IS A STATE OF MIND

What most people don't realize is that nutritional needs do *not* decline with age. Just because you're not hungry doesn't mean you shouldn't eat. It means you need to take a walk around the block to pump up your appetite. The reality, according to Rasmussen, is "that the older you get, the more important it is to consume foods that are high in *nutrient density*—that is, packed with vitamins, minerals and other health-promoting nutritional factors."

No matter how old you are, or how much time has passed since you last exercised or felt healthy, it's never too late for change. LaLanne says, "Getting out of shape is like a thief in the night that sneaks up on you. I always tell people that it is never too late. I tell them about the folks in their nineties who doubled their strength and endurance."

Guideposts writer Harold Hostetler isn't ninety, but he too had to realize that getting healthy was more a matter of attitude than physical aptitude:

> There were times when I wondered if I was slowing down. Or was it the fact that, in the three years since joining the Medicare generation, I just wanted to "take it easy"? I knew I needed exercise, but I'd fallen out of the habit, often putting it off as too strenuous or boring. No wonder I could no longer walk two miles in thirty minutes as I had before retiring.
>
> I knew something had to be done, so I vowed to walk at least five times a week, early in the day, before the sun heated up our Southern California neighborhood. I measured off a two-mile course. Each morning I donned my shorts and walking shoes, set my wristwatch to tick off the seconds, and strode off. I warmed up for five minutes, walked for thirty, then cooled down for five minutes.
>
> As the weeks passed, I began to thank and praise God as I walked. I enjoyed smelling flowers, saying hello to neighbors and other walkers, watching commuters leave for work and seeing children head off to school. Gradually I came closer to my goal of two miles in thirty minutes. Eventually, I reached it.
>
> Then one morning my pace seemed faster. A couple jogging

by called out, "Hey, you're really moving!" Me? A fortyish woman walking in the opposite direction eyed me and commented, "I guess I'd better speed up!" And she did.

When I crossed the two-mile mark, I looked at my watch and did a double take. I'd made a quantum leap in speed: twenty-eight minutes! So it wasn't my age slowing me down; it was my attitude. And that's something I could change. I continued walking for two more minutes, exhilarated. And feeling younger than I had in years.

SIMPLICITY MADE SIMPLE

LIGHTEN YOUR BURDEN BY LIFTING WEIGHTS. According to Dave Pearson, an exercise scientist, "The top reason to pursue strength training is because we lose muscle mass as we get older. It doesn't require the commitment of a bodybuilder. You can train twice a week to keep the muscle mass you have." It's also a superior strategy for women who want to maintain bone density. Research shows that strength training can improve mobility and balance well into our nineties. Dixie Stanforth, a personal trainer and exercise science instructor at the University of Texas in Austin, believes that we shouldn't be choosing between aerobic exercises and lifting weights. "Do a little of both. You will realize better results if you don't skip the weight lifting."

Give your brain a workout! A panel of experts on memory, stress and multitasking attended AARP's annual "Life@50+" National Event and Expo. They agreed that stress and multitasking can take a toll on memory, but that leading a "brain-healthy lifestyle" can help—at any age. The panelists said that the cornerstones of a brain-healthy lifestyle are physical and cognitive exercise, together with a plan for managing stress, and eating a healthy diet rich in antioxidants and omega-3 fatty acids. Dr. Gordon of the panel said, "Mental aerobics can have as great an impact and as high a yield as physical aerobics. Do something that you are interested in and that you find useful. This will really help expand your mind, and can have tremendous effects." Gordon also said we should be comforted by the fact that **BRAINPOWER CAN BE IMPROVED AT ANY AGE**. In fact, Gordon says, "Some lessons of neuroscience are actually rediscovering what educators and teachers have known forever, which is that you can build up mental skills. It's what we call learning."[12]

TAKE A NAP AND SHARPEN YOUR BRAIN. Who knew that simply sleeping could re-energize my brain? New studies contradict the common belief that daytime naps make it harder to sleep at night. A recent study had persons ages fifty-five to eighty-five take naps on some days but not on others. The length of the naps ranged from twelve minutes to two hours. On the day following the nap, the individuals scored better on tests of reasoning, reaction time and perception than they did after non-nap days. And on nap days, they slept no less at night.

WORKOUTS SHOULD INCLUDE THREE TYPES OF EXERCISE for overall fitness. They are calisthenics for flexibility, weight training for strength and aerobic exercise for cardiovascular health. However, the routines should be tailored to your abilities. If you are frail or overweight, avoid exercises that require a high level of agility, balance or coordination. Focus on supportive exercises such as weight-stack machines or exercises done in water. If you are easily bored, look for exercises that require a lot of movement, such as an elliptical trainer or rowing machine. Also, remember that no one approach does it all.

I love Pilates for the stretching and strengthening but it does not include aerobic benefits, which is why I either attend a thirty-five minute core-cardio class or walk for aerobic exercise. Tai chi is a wonderful option that is gentle and excellent for gaining flexibility, balance and reducing stress. Because tai chi requires the participants to breathe very slowly, it aids in circulation and is more nourishing to the inner organs. It can also help lower blood pressure. The isometric pressure on the muscles and joints strengthens without the pounding of aerobic exercise, which is why it is so popular with seniors.

TRY SOME BRAIN BUILDERS: Instead of watching TV sitting in your lounge chair, try sitting on an oversized exercise ball instead. It will help strengthen your sense of balance while challenging both parts of your brain—your left brain as you concentrate on the exercise and your creative right brain as you take in new information from television. Exercise your nondominant hand by changing sides for simple activities like brushing your teeth or dialing the phone to strengthen little-used neural pathways. Dance to the music—a little "do-si-do" can help protect against dementia because it requires multiple mental and physical skills. Play cards or board games—and don't forget crossword puzzles. They all give your brain a vigorous workout.

Thank You, Lord, for keeping me alert to the many things there are to enjoy each day. Forgive me for idle moments, and remind me to get outside and breathe in the freshness of each new day. Amen.

Live Happily Ever After

But the fruit of the Spirit is love, joy, peace,
patience, kindness, goodness, faithfulness,
gentleness and self-control. . . .

—GALATIANS 5:22–23 (NIV)

Joy clearly comes from the Holy Spirit. As believers, we find joy in obeying Christ's commands, and when we are obedient even life's trials will not take away our joy. The New Testament uses three Greek words for joy: *Eurphrainõ*, which carries a sense of merrymaking and has both a secular and a religious connotation; *chairõ*, the most common word, which describes an inner feeling of pleasure, satisfaction or well-being; and *agalliaõ*, which comes closest to the Old Testament sense of jubilation or worship. Scripture usually sets joy apart from mere happiness. It is rooted not in things but in God's covenant love for us. Such joy is supernaturally produced as we look to our future with confidence, knowing God and goodness will triumph. The joy of *chairõ* is readily available to all of us simply by being obedient to Christ. Yet, many of us know Christians who are not joyful—and that is not only sad, but it can also have a negative effect on their life in general.

In her book *Retire Smart, Retire Happy: Finding Your True Path in Life*, Nancy Schlossberg reports the work of Martin Seligman, who studied the different ways people react to negative, uncontrollable or bad events. "According to Seligman, those who feel optimistic about their own power to control at least some portions of their lives tend to experience less depression. Optimism, he claims, is good for your performance, and good for your overall health."[13]

You will find similar results if you simply ask the real experts—those that have lived long and happy lives such as Agnes Dill, age ninety-one, from Albuquerque, New Mexico. When asked, Agnes said that being optimistic is her secret to living a stress-reduced life. She was the first American Indian woman to go to New Mexico Highlands University. Even though macular degeneration prevents her from doing many of the things she used to enjoy, "I'm very optimistic about life," she says. "I accept things as they happen and make them better if I can. Most days, I don't feel my age. I just feel pretty happy." Grace Nunery, age eighty-six, of Indianapolis says her secret to a stress-free life is praying. "I don't worry about anything, and I pray about everything," she says.

And Thais Crowell, age ninety-one, says her secret is playing the drums. What she loves most about music is the feeling of inspiration it invokes. After moving into a retirement community ten years ago, she signed up for drumming lessons and was immediately hooked. "I feel myself relaxing right away when I start drumming," she says. While learning anything new has been proven to beat stress, music has a special ability to calm people. Decades of research have shown that listening to music can lower blood pressure and heart rate. A new study at the Mind-Body Wellness Center in Pennsylvania also found that playing music can significantly reduce stress.

HOLD ON TO HAPPY THOUGHTS

Living happily ever after obviously requires the right attitude. What, you might ask, can you do if you are a pessimist? What if aging seems negative and filled with more losses than opportunities? Seligman actually trains people to be optimists. He found that those who receive this training are in better health than those not participating in his sessions. But you can train yourself as well. In his book, *Learned Optimism*, Seligman shows readers how to dispute their negative thoughts. You can argue with yourself. For example, every time you begin to think negatively and hear yourself say, "I can't," simply argue with yourself. Ask yourself what is preventing you from doing what you want. Pretend you were arguing with someone else who kept saying, "I can't." What would you tell them? Then begin to tell it to yourself. This technique is not meant to be used to argue yourself into a falsely optimistic view, but to help you learn to realistically reframe an event.

Happiness is so critical to our well-being that the January 17, 2005, issue of *Time* magazine was devoted entirely to the subject. In that issue, University of California psychologist Sonja Lyubomirsky offered eight practical suggestions to lift your level of happiness, based on research findings by her and others: Count your blessings, practice acts of kindness, savor life's joys, thank a mentor, learn to forgive, invest time and energy in family and friends, take care of your body, and develop strategies for coping with stress and hardships. These suggestions sound remarkably similar to the fruits of the spirit listed in Galatians 5:22–23.

The simple secret to a long and happy life is to think happy thoughts and use the power of positive thinking as Guideposts writer Arthur Gordon learned from his friend Jack:

> "Attitudes," a great American psychiatrist once said, "are more important than fact." I thought of this the other day when I went to see a longtime friend in the hospital. Jack had been a marvelous athlete as a young man and an energetic civic leader in the years that followed. Now the sudden onset of a serious kidney disorder had left him dependent on dialysis machines just to stay alive.
>
> I knew how difficult this drastically curtailed existence must be for him and tried to express the sympathy I felt. But he waved my words aside. "We all go through stages in life," he said. "Here I am, and I can't say I enjoy these surroundings. What I try to focus on is the fun I've had getting here. The Lord gave me so many good times that there's no end to the happy memories I can summon up. When I do, this hospital room just fades away."
>
> *The fun I've had getting here*. I wish I had a calendar with that phrase inscribed at the top of every page. Even on dark days, it would be a reminder of how many sunny ones there have been. A reminder too to be grateful to the One Who made those happy times possible.

SIMPLICITY MADE SIMPLE

Adopt a good attitude. **GOOD ATTITUDES ASSURE HAPPINESS AND SUCCESS IN LIFE** while poor attitudes bring failure, pain and sadness. The first teaching that Jesus shared with His disciples was to deal with attitudes. The Beatitudes each start with the word for blessed, which means happy or fortunate. According to Jesus these eight attitudes are what make for true happiness and success: They are humility, mournfulness, modesty, ambitiousness, compassion, sincerity, peacekeeping and perseverance. The promises for adopting these attitudes include comfort, fulfillment, inheriting the kingdom and seeing God.

Temper your anger. According to Michael Roizen, an internist, anesthesiologist and preventive gerontologist at the University of Chicago, studies show that genetics accounts for less than thirty percent of all effects of aging. That means we can control seventy percent of the aging process. He says, "**ANGER IS A MUCH BIGGER DEAL THAN HIGH CHOLESTEROL**. Only fifty percent of people with high cholesterol have heart attacks. Get your anger under control or you'll get heart disease."

REDUCE YOUR PERCEPTION OF STRESS. Roizen says another factor that adds years to one's age is traumatic life events. Three or more traumatic life events, such as death in a family or divorce, in the same year can make one age as much as thirty-two years. With proper strategies for coping in place for stress reduction, the additional aging drops to just two years. He suggests building strong social networks as a way of reducing stress. Researchers have actually found that constant stress causes the telomeres—tiny caps on the cells' chromosomes that govern cell regeneration—to get smaller. When a cell's telomeres get too short, the cell stops dividing and eventually dies. The greater you *perceive* your stress level to be, the shorter your telomeres will be. Stress doesn't age us nearly as much as the perceptions of stress. Thomas Perls, an associate professor of medicine at Boston University, said, "It isn't the amount of stress that matters but how you manage it." In fact, a number of the centenarians that Dr. Perls has studied have endured plenty of stress. After all, they lived through the Great Depression and World Wars I and II—not to mention the usual number of divorces, deaths of loved ones and job losses. "Yet they don't seem to internalize it," Perls says, "They just let it go."

MAKE FRIENDS AND STAY INVOLVED. Happy older people don't care how old they are. What counts is what they're doing, thinking and enjoying. One study found that people who rarely thought about their age were more satisfied than those who did.

Lord, I'm not concerned about being older, I'm just happy to have one more day to get to know You better. And each day I pray to make more room for Your "be-attitudes" in exchange for my bad attitudes. Amen.

Putting Your Affairs in Order

For to me, to live is Christ and to die is gain. If I am to go on living in the body, this will mean fruitful labor for me. Yet what shall I choose? I do not know! I am torn between the two: I desire to depart and be with Christ, which is better by far; but it is more necessary for you that I remain in the body.

—PHILIPPIANS 1:21–24 (NIV)

Paul expected at the end of his life to "depart and be with Christ, which is better by far." He knew that God had prepared a heavenly dwelling that he would receive when he died. Despite this hope-filled view of death, it remains a terribly distorted perspective of what God originally intended for all of us. From a biblical viewpoint, death is *un*natural, and the whole universe strains to be liberated from death's bondage. Perhaps that's why we are so resistant to even talking about death, and even more reluctant to prepare for it. But getting our affairs in order is necessary, no matter how uncomfortable it is.

What's interesting is that older parents usually do want to talk about their end-of-life preparations, but it is their children who avoid those conversations. A new survey of five hundred parents in their seventies, and 450 adult children, ages forty-five to sixty-five, found that three-quarters of the parents said they were "very comfortable" talking about their estate and other affairs. But only forty-five percent of the children felt the same way. The survey also found that as a result of families not talking about these issues, only half of the children surveyed thought that their parents even had a living will or durable power of attorney, even though two-thirds of the parents said they had these tools in place.[15]

Maureen Mohyde, director of Hartford's corporate gerontology group said, "Adult children are uncomfortable with these conversations, because they deny that at some point their parents will be gone. But parents want to talk about it, even if it's just talking about passing along one keepsake. Those keepsakes matter a lot, and frankly are what families wind up fighting about." I found it interesting that even among the parents who have talked to their children, the survey results found that a lot of parents have spoken to one child but not all of their offspring.

TELL YOUR LOVED ONES WHAT YOU WANT

The painful debate in state and federal courts over what to do—or not to do—for Terri Schiavo, who had remained on life support for years, certainly should have inspired all of us to think about decisions we should be making while we are of sound mind and body. The Schiavo situation should also make it apparent that age doesn't matter. Everyone over the age of eighteen should have a will and a living will. Paul Malley, president of Aging with

Dignity says, “You don’t want your first conversation about end-of-life issues to be in a hospital emergency room. If you’re eighteen or older, you should think about these questions, get a legally valid document, and talk about your choices with your family and doctor.”

Too often, we avoid such discussions with family simply because we assume they will be complicated and upsetting. The reality is that filling out paperwork is easier than having a conversation with your loved ones. And by keeping things simple and straightforward, you can make the process much easier for everyone. One way to keep it simple is to use the Five Wishes form that is available from Aging with Dignity’s Web site at www.agingwithdignity.org or by calling (888) 594-7437. Their twelve-page document prompts individuals to consider five questions and issues: who your health-care agent should be (the person making decisions if you are unable to do so); what kind of medical treatment you want in various situations; how comfortable you wish to be (addressing issues like pain medication); how you want people to treat you (would you prefer to die at home?); and what you want your loved ones to know (where you wish to be buried, for instance).

Once you have filled out a living will, it is critical that you discuss it with your family, doctor and health-care agent. As I went through this process, I found out in talking about it with my husband that we have very different views on what should or should not be done under extreme circumstances. It made me realize that even though it’s in writing and we have discussed it, it will still be very difficult for my husband to honor my wishes. That means we need to continue talking about it so that he can slowly adjust and, it is hoped, be able to accept my terms for the end of my life. The good news is that by beginning this conversation now, while we are both healthy, we can take the time we need to accept each other’s desires.

Perhaps we simply need to look to Jesus for an example of preparing for the end. That's what Guideposts writer Eleanor Sass learned when a dear friend was nearing the end of her life:

> This was Jesus' time of preparation. He knew that in just two days His work on earth would be finished and He would return to His Father. So He used the time to prepare His followers for what lay ahead.
>
> "Let not your hearts be troubled," He counseled. "In my Father's house are many rooms" (John 14:1–2, RSV).
>
> To me these are some of the most reassuring words in the Bible. Even today, two thousand years later, they never fail to bring comfort.
>
> I remember when my dear friend and colleague Nancy Schraffenberger was suffering with a terminal respiratory ailment. Every breath was an effort for her. It was painful to watch. At Nancy's funeral, a minister, who had been close to her during her final days, told us that at one point she pleaded, "Teach me how to die." Nancy knew her death was imminent and she wanted to prepare for it.
>
> There are different ways of preparing. Some people make wills, others put their affairs in order. Yet all we really need to do is have faith in the promise of Jesus, powerful promises He made to His followers so long ago. In His words were the calmness, dignity, courage and confidence to face death. They can do the same for us.

Seek the advice of an elder law attorney. These professionals have gained expertise from long hours of study to holistically advise recommendations specific to your family and your assets. The four basic documents that are almost always recommended as the starting point are the Will, the Living Will, the Durable Power of Attorney for Healthcare and the Durable Power of Attorney. The Will makes probate easy. Probate is the process that pays all of your last legal debts and distributes your assets where you designate. The Living Will indicates to family members and physicians which medical treatments are—and are not—desired in the event that you are unable to make your own decisions. Peter Strauss, coauthor of *Complete Retirement Survival Guide*, notes that **SPECIFICITY IS CRUCIAL** when it comes to drafting a successful Living Will. For example, do not say "this document becomes effective when I have a terminal illness." Instead say, "If I have no cognitive function that allows me to communicate meaningfully with other people and no reasonable chance that my condition will improve . . ." This type of language clarifies what you mean by "incapacitated." Also, don't talk about "heroic measures." Instead, list specific measures—such as antibiotics, CPR, dialysis, feeding tubes, hydration, pacemakers, respirators, surgery and transfusions of blood or blood products—that you do or do not want. Being specific about your desires takes a huge burden off of loved ones.

THINK CAREFULLY ABOUT WHOM YOU CHOOSE AS YOUR HEALTH-CARE AGENT. Arthur Caplan, director of University of Pennsylvania's Center for Bioethics in Philadelphia, says that a health-care proxy permits a trusted "agent," usually a spouse, adult child or other close relative or friend, to express your wishes if you cannot communicate on your own and to interpret those wishes if there is any uncertainty. Review both your Living Will and your Durable Power of Attorney for Healthcare every two years. Make changes that are appropriate, notify everyone concerned and be sure to give them a new copy.

PREPLAN YOUR FUNERAL. Making funeral arrangements close to the time of need can be stressful and confusing. By preplanning you can have your specific wishes known in advance. However, be aware that there are plenty of people looking to take advantage of seniors wishing to preplan. Joshua Slocum of the Funeral Consumers' Alliance said, "The first thing everyone has to remember, when you walk into a funeral home and begin talking about funeral arrangements, the funeral director must give you a printed price list. That is a federal regulation. If you walk into a funeral home and such a list is not given to you when you begin the discussion or anyone seems cagey, that's not a good sign." Slocum also said that although it is a good idea to preplan, it is a very bad idea to pay for your funeral in advance, "because all fifty states have different regulations on how well or how poorly your money is protected. It's something you should do as a family and say, "'What do we want, what do we expect, what are we looking for' and that way you don't get gouged." The Federal Trade Commission suggests shopping around in advance, asking for a price list, resisting pressure to buy, avoiding emotional spending and recognizing your rights. In other words, be a smart consumer. Planning ahead allows you the time to comparison shop and creates an opportunity for family discussion.

Hire a funeral concierge. This is a new idea that might just take off. **FUNERAL CONCIERGES HELP FAMILIES PLAN A FUNERAL**, even negotiating terms and prices with funeral homes. For one family that was scattered from San Francisco to New York who were struggling to make arrangements for their eighty-three-year-old mother's funeral in Atlanta, the concierge service was a blessing. "Relying on the concierge gave us time to console ourselves, fly to Atlanta and talk about what we wanted to say at Mother's service." Everests' concierge service said, "We work as advocates for the families," noting that the company received no fees or commissions from the industry. "We ask our clients what they want, then we find the requested services at the best prices. Our whole mission is to make it easier for someone to plan a funeral, either beforehand or at the time of death," said Terry Hemeyer, a managing director for Houston-based Service Corporation International.

Father, when I think of the promises that You hold for me in heaven, I become eager to see Your face. Your love removes my fear of death. But, Lord, keep me brave enough to live well all the days that You have appointed for me to enjoy on earth. May my life here demonstrate the glory of Your goodness even after I depart. Amen.

PART FIVE

Simply Satisfied

EMBRACING RETIREMENT means expecting new ways of looking at old habits, such as the way we spend our time. God has an entirely new perspective to reveal to us through this sacred spiritual journey of life after work. Now is the time to use all that we have learned over the years to share our faith with others, and *now* is the moment that time is finally on our side. Many times when doors close to old routines, such as the task of raising children, working and then coping with an empty nest, we can lose sight of the wonderful opportunities that now appear ahead of us. God has a purpose for keeping us on earth these extra years. There is still much to do, so stir up your prayer life and finish these final pages of reflection on how to enjoy a simply satisfying life.

A Spiritual Journey

Do not conform any longer to the pattern of this world,
but be transformed by the renewing of your mind. . . .

—ROMANS 12:2 (NIV)

As we replace our old way of thinking and adopt an entirely new perspective from God's point of view, we'll begin to recognize God's will for our lives, including our later years. The goal of aging should not be to only maintain health and financial wellness—instead, we must learn to think differently about our approach to aging, seeing it as a new and unique stage in life. Rather than simply trying to extend our youth, we should consider aging as a spiritual journey. Drew Leder, a professor of philosophy at Loyola University in Maryland and author of the workbook, *Spiritual Passages: Embracing Life's Sacred Journey*, drew upon the beliefs of many different cultures to build a model of aging as an opportunity for spiritual growth.

Leder discovered that most sacred traditions emphasize one or two roles for older adults: embarking on a quest for personal spiritual growth or mentoring the younger generation. As he researched, he discovered, for example, that Native American cultures expected older people to become elders, to use their accumulated knowledge and wisdom to advise and guide the tribe. Leder calls this approach to aging "spiritual eldering." Leder believes that even elderly individuals who are ill and unable to volunteer or travel to spiritual retreats can find solace in the spiritual eldering process. He says, "Even if you don't stay healthy, you can use that as part of your spiritual growth. Disability causes people to seek out social and spiritual wholeness." In fact, an inward spiritual journey can help ill or disabled people to learn to come to terms with death and dying, relieving anxiety about mortality. Besides, no matter how ill you are, you can still pray.

Tony Evans, author of *Life Essentials: For Knowing God Better, Experiencing God Deeper, Loving God More*, wrote "God says that your job and mine as believers is to be billboards advertising His grace to a lost world. And He wants us to grow so that we can display Him more. As we get up in the morning our prayer should be, 'Lord, grow me today so I can show You as being bigger and clearer to the people around me.'" Second Peter 3:18 implies that spiritual growth requires two important ingredients: grace and knowledge of our Lord and Savior Jesus Christ.

THERE'S ALWAYS SOMETHING NEW TO LEARN ABOUT GOD

We all know that aging is not for sissies. But as my departed dear friend Edward used to say, "It sure beats the alternative." Living a life of purpose and growth requires optimism and joyful hope. Our hope is Christ, our optimism is a choice we make in how we view our lives. We can grumble about our aches and pains. We can be content to simply relax and take it easy. Or we can choose to keep growing and offer our lives as a living sacrifice to God by embarking on a spiritual journey for the rest of our days. When we do, we will realize that our work for the Lord is never done, regardless of age, health or finances as Guideposts writer Mary Ruth Howes learned from her own father:

> During one of my weekend visits to my ninety-four-year-old father's retirement home in Pennsylvania, Daddy kept gamely trying to stay upright, independent and awake. The afternoon that I left to drive back to New Jersey we had a time of prayer as we usually did. Daddy, as always, asked for a safe trip for me, and then added, "Lord, please help me to catch up on my work. I've gotten so far behind."
>
> I chuckled a bit to myself as I drove home, wondering, *What work is he talking about?*
>
> In the next weeks, I discovered what he meant. He was behind in his prayer schedule. For him, prayer was his work. Every day, every week, he had gone through his overflowing loose-leaf notebook filled with letters and prayer requests from friends, missionaries and missions around the world. As he prayed over every person, every request, he would mark the date.
>
> One reason Daddy had been willing to give up his independence and move to the retirement home was to have more time to pray. But now, he didn't have the energy to go through the book or even to read the new letters that came. Yet as his strength waned and his tongue thickened, he would phone friends to find out how they were and what he could pray for as he sat immobilized.

"How much your dad's prayers and interest in us have meant" was the comment that came again and again after his death. "He was a true prayer warrior."

What a legacy!

SIMPLICITY MADE SIMPLE

Recognize that **SPIRITUAL TRANSFORMATION IS A LONG-TERM ENDEAVOR** that requires a partnership between you and God. Pastor Chris Benjamin of the West-Ark Church of Christ in Fort Smith, Arkansas, says, "I liken it to crossing an ocean. Some people try, day after day, to be good, to become spiritually mature. That's like taking a rowboat across the ocean. It's exhausting and usually unsuccessful. Others have given up trying and throw themselves entirely on 'relying on God's grace.' They're like drifters on a raft. They do nothing but hang on and hope God gets them there. Neither trying nor drifting is effective in bringing about spiritual transformation. A better image is the sailboat, which, if it moves at all, is a gift of the wind. We can't control the wind, but a good sailor discerns where the wind is blowing and adjusts the sails accordingly."

LIVE YOUR LIFE AS AN OFFERING. An offering must be *given*. It is not something you keep for your own use. For example, you don't put an offering in the church basket and then after the service take it back again for your own use, do you? Being an offering means that you are willing to take some risk. Lynn Miller, a traveling stewardship teacher for Mennonite Mutual Aid, says, "Think about it in terms of your own life, especially in view of retirement.

Why would you go to all the trouble of developing career skills and financial resources to save them up for a 'comfortable retirement' for yourself? Church treasurers don't take your offerings to the bank and put them in twenty-year certificates of deposit. They put them in checking accounts because they plan on using them. It is the same for the gift of life. It is something to be used up in the ministry of God."

Feed yourself on God's Word. In *Life Essentials*, Tony Evans said, "If you are pursuing a relationship with Jesus Christ and are passionately committed to bringing Him glory, your spiritual life will grow at a speed you never imagined possible. The reason is that your growth will take care of itself as you **FEED YOUR SOUL ON GOD AND HIS WORD**, the way a child's growth takes care of itself as he feeds and exercises his body." If you are not growing and maturing, it may be that God isn't getting the glory He seeks and deserves in your life. God only expands those who bring Him praise.

Make the right choice. Plato said, "The spiritual eyesight improves as the physical eyesight declines." The choice to **FULLY INTEGRATE YOUR FAITH INTO YOUR LIFE** and follow God's plan is yours to make each day. By focusing internally you become a central player in a new and exciting adventure of spiritual growth and development. Diane D'Agostino, a certified retirement coach, says, "Healthy resolution of the spiritual challenges of the second half of your life requires that your lifestyle choices acquire new meaning. This emerging sense of spiritual empowerment allows you to take command of your thoughts, your feelings and your decisions in ways that are identifiably different from what was required in previous years." God has a very special plan for you, whatever you do—"do it all in the name of the Lord" (Colossians 3:17).

Lord, I believe that this is a time of blessing in my life—
a time to grow in grace and knowledge of You. Fill each day
with the wind of Your Holy Spirit and keep me sailing
in a direction that brings me closer to You. Amen.

Dealing with Grief and Loss

In this you greatly rejoice, though now for a little while
you may have had to suffer grief in all kinds of trials.
These have come so that your faith—of greater worth
than gold, which perishes even though refined by fire—
may be proved genuine and may result in praise,
glory and honor when Jesus Christ is revealed.

—1 PETER 1:6–7 (NIV)

Grief is an intense emotional suffering, often caused by some loss or disaster. First Peter 1:3–9 presents truths that should bring us comfort in times of grief. After all, we have an inheritance in heaven, and our trials and suffering reveal our genuine character of faith and result in praise, honor and glory of God. And we have access to the love of Jesus that fills us with an inexpressible joy, regardless of our circumstances.

Yet, every day in the United States, seventeen adults over the age of sixty-five commit suicide—the highest suicide rate of any demographic group in the country. The leading cause of suicide is depression. According to one study, twenty to twenty-five percent of the elderly in nursing homes are clinically depressed. In an article entitled "Depression and Suicide in the Elderly: What You Can Do," Elisa Thomas, a specialist in human development and aging issues, says that their reasons are often despair, the desire to escape suffering, economic and financial problems, fear of burdening family members and, of course, loss. They grieve over the loss of a spouse, friends, independence and even the loss of their familiar environment.

People of all ages experience loss in their lives. What makes loss so significant in later life is that it often occurs within a short time period and with greater intensity than in earlier life, according to Tina Rains, a minister to the aging for Wisconsin Lutheran Child and Family Service. Harriet Rzetelny, author of *Emotional Stresses in Later Life*, says, "These losses occur at a time when a person's physiological reserves and opportunities for replacement, substitution and gratification are at their lowest." What we must remember is that the intensity of the loss is directly related to the value we place on that which is lost. Losing a spouse or a dear friend later in life is intense because we place so much value on those relationships. As a result, coping with loss remains the most significant developmental task of the aging process.

Rzetelny breaks down the losses of later life into four categories: the aging process itself; health, illness and disease; the death of others; and social and environmental losses. The aging process is gradual, taking place over a long period of time. Few of us are emotionally and psychologically prepared for our bodies to whither away. Illness and disease cause chronic impairments that add to our aging burdens. Blindness, hearing impairment/ deafness or a deterioration of some body part increases with age. It also takes more time to gain strength and recover from illness as we age. Almost half of the elderly have illnesses that interfere to some degree with their ability to engage in normal activities of daily living.

The loss of significant people is particularly stressful as we age because we are unlikely to establish new relationships in the future. Each loss deprives us of a source of caring and a support system. Rains says, "The importance of quality relationships in the lives of aging people cannot be overestimated." Rains also points out that the loss of a significant person can mean a major change in the life of the survivor. This is especially true if we have depended on that person for our daily care. That loss may force us to move from our home into a nursing home or other assisted living situation. Experiencing the death of family and friends can also bring us face-to-face with our own mortality. As we age, we need to be able to express our sadness over all these losses in order to work through the grieving process.

LOOK FOR SOMEONE TO ENCOURAGE

We must all realize that aging followers of a religion need the same kind of support and encouragement to go on living full lives as persons without faith. Of course, we are aware that faith in the Lord secures us a heavenly reward and provides a keen sense of comfort. But the reality of great loss and the disruption it brings to our lives cannot be ignored. As Tina Rains put it, "We need to be sure therefore to provide both the scriptural comfort and emotional support they need." Remember, faith without works is dead. What good does it do to say to someone in depression to "cheer up," if we aren't willing to sit and let him talk about his loss and grief?

We are all in this together. Second Corinthians 1:4 (KJV) says "that we may be able to comfort them which are in any trouble, by the comfort wherewith we ourselves are comforted of God." Together, we can find comfort as Guideposts writer Arthur Gordon discovered when he was just a college student:

> Grief is something that all of us encounter from time to time. Most people eventually put it aside and go on with living. But some find that difficult to do. What's the remedy when long-held grief leaves a person shrouded in darkness?
>
> Years ago, I was traveling in Spain with two other college students. In Malaga, we stayed in a *pensione*, a private home that took in guests. It was comfortable enough, but strangely somber. The owner never smiled. His wife wore black. In the living room was a grand piano, but it was always closed. The maid told us that the wife had been a concert pianist, but three years ago her teenage son had died. She had not touched the piano since.
>
> We carefree youngsters gave little thought on this. One afternoon when we came home full of high spirits, one of my companions sat down at the piano and began to play, rather badly, a college song that we all began to sing. Almost at once, the maid rushed in looking distracted. Behind her came the husband frantically motioning to us to desist. At the same time, another door opened and there stood the señora, tall and pale and silent.
>
> Our music died away. We were horribly embarrassed. We didn't know what to say or do. Then suddenly the señora

smiled. She came forward, pushed my friend aside, sat down at the piano and began to play the triumphal march from *Aida*, wonderful, soaring music that seemed to fill the whole house and drive the shadows away. What had happened? She had felt sorry for *us*, not for herself, and that sudden warmth had melted the ice around her heart.

Concern for others. Perhaps that's the best prescription and antidote for grief—if we're wise enough to use it.

SIMPLICITY MADE SIMPLE

Be aware and **KNOW THE SIGNS OF DEPRESSION**. They occur in many forms such as fatigue and loss of energy, frequent physical complaints and insomnia; diminished ability to think or concentrate and recurrent thoughts of death or suicidal ideas; feelings of worthlessness; sudden weight gain or loss; lethargy and loss of interest in formerly pleasurable activities. Another red flag may be the depressed individual's declaring that he or she is a "burden" to others. Too often, we misinterpret these symptoms as normal signs of aging. For many older people, the losses can become a continuous part of their lives, making it difficult for them or others to recognize the differences between natural grief and clinical depression. Remember, depression can lead to suicide, and by recognizing the signs early, you may intervene in time.

Encourage discussion. If you are dealing with depressed people, it is important to encourage dialogue about their feelings. **SHOW AN INTEREST AND A WILLINGNESS TO LISTEN** by asking questions and sharing their sorrow. Don't offer false comfort. It doesn't help the grieving person when you say, "It was for the best," or "You'll get over it in time." Instead, offer a simple expression of sorrow and take time to listen.

SEEK OUTSIDE HELP WHEN NECESSARY. If you or someone you know seems overwhelmed with grief that is too much to bear, seek professional assistance to help work through the grief. It's a sign of strength and wisdom, not weakness, to obtain help. Encourage professional help when necessary. There are several different ways that professionals can assist. Counseling—which is simply talking with a trained psychotherapist—can help older adults better understand their feelings and develop skills for meeting the challenges of aging. Cognitive therapy helps to change negative thinking patterns that occur during depression, such as a sense of worthlessness or inappropriate guilt. Behavioral therapy focuses on the person's daily experiences that contribute to stress. Interpersonal therapy helps deal with relationships and role problems that contribute to stress. If there is a biochemical imbalance, the best approach is one that combines medication (often termed *psychotropics*, or drugs acting on the mind) with therapy. When carefully prescribed and monitored by a physician (usually a psychiatrist but sometimes a primary care doctor), medication can relieve symptoms of depression in three to six weeks. It may be continued for extended periods of time.

SEEK OUT CARING PEOPLE. Find relatives or friends who can understand your loss. Join a support group with others who are experiencing similar losses. A friend of mine has a father-in-law who is ninety-two. When his father was widowed a few years ago, they found a cleaning lady to help him out. She has turned out to be a tremendous help and a friend. She comes two days a week to help him with cooking, cleaning, etc. But most important, she is there simply to listen and chat with him. Poor eyesight and loss of friends often gets him down, but his "cleaning lady" has helped to keep his "blue days" to a minimum.

Lord, help me to be sensitive to my friends who are also aging and facing changes. Prompt me when someone needs a phone call to be cheered or encouraged. I realize that in lifting the spirits of others, I, too, will find reason to celebrate each new day. Amen.

Giving Your Time

Life is no brief candle to me. It is a sort of
splendid torch which I have got a hold of for the moment,
and I want to make it burn as brightly as possible
before handing it on to future generations.

—GEORGE BERNARD SHAW, IRISH DRAMATIST AND LITERARY CRITIC (1856–1950)

I love the concept of making your life burn as brightly as possible before passing it on. Yet for many years, people thought of retirement as a time of slowing down, a dimming of life. The good news is that things are changing. According to Carl Ericson, a spokesman for Volunteers of America (www.voa.org), the largest growing volunteer segment is now the fifty-five-and-over crowd, which makes up about twenty-five percent of the 32,000 volunteers at this organization.

In a new trend, retirees are volunteering as missionaries. According to CBS Radio Network's *The Osgood File*, a growing number of religious groups are encouraging retired people to use their golden years to serve God. Lloyd Reeb, a leader with the Retirees for God movement and author of *From Success to Significance*, attributes the growing interest in mission work among retirees to a "perfect storm" of three changes that happened at once. First, the baby boomer generation is getting older, with an expected thirteen million of us retiring between 2002 and 2012. Second, the boomers are the first generation in which most people, upon turning fifty, will still have thirty years of living left. Third, Reeb believes, the baby boomers have typically sought to do more than earn money to enjoy a comfortable suburban life. We are not simply going to retire to a golf course. We have always wanted to make a difference, and retirement seems to be the perfect time to make the most impact with *our* time.

GOD HAS WORK THAT ONLY YOU CAN DO

In the past, mission groups primarily targeted youth, but they too have changed their focus to capitalize on the experience and maturity of the baby boomers. The result is a number of emerging new groups that are devoted to this older segment, including The Finishers, Halftime, Focus on the Family's Focus over Fifty group, CitiReach, Second Half Ministries, and the Navigators. These groups offer Web sites, workshops and mentoring to help retired and semiretired folks find their niche in mission work. The Finishers, for example, have six thousand people registered within their database so they can easily match skills and interests to mission projects to ensure a good fit and success.

Their director, Nelson Malwitz, says, "We know we've placed over six hundred people in ministry but the ripple effects are even bigger because many more have gotten involved in short-term or part-time projects, and have enlisted the involvement of friends." Malwitz says that Scripture inspires the work of The Finishers—the name of the group comes from the words of the apostle Paul: "I consider my life worth nothing to me, if only I may finish the race and complete the task the Lord Jesus had given me—the task of testifying to the gospel of God's grace" (Acts 20:24). Malwitz says the idea of "finishing well" speaks to those who are in their later years.

Missions are changing too. At one time we simply thought of missionaries as those serving in the medical fields or people with skills in construction and agriculture. But today, mission projects are taking advantage of retirees' business management and leadership skills as well as helping people in countries that are in transition. For example, one retiree has set up two-week, intensive training workshops in the Ukraine to teach business management skills to college students. The project has been so successful that they have now turned to The Finishers in search of additional retirees to recruit more teachers.

Volunteering your time does not necessarily mean you must stay within your original field or scope of work either. Sometimes trying something new is just what the doctor ordered to make your life more meaningful. One gentleman named Jack found himself in early retirement as a result of downsizing. At first, he took on some consulting work in his own field, and then he tried his hand at selling insurance. He also worked in a local hardware store and even ran for public office. Yet nothing felt right until he finally decided to pursue his pastime as work. Jack always loved gardening. His yard was the envy of neighbors. So he started a small seasonal lawn care business. This job not only kept him in shape, but it was something he excelled at and truly enjoyed. Others also benefited from it, like the elderly lady who said he made it possible for her to stay in her home because Jack took care of her yard for her.

I believe that God has called us specifically for this time and place. Regardless of our talents and abilities, God has a purpose in ministry for each of us. The Church of the Saviour in Washington, D.C., is also convinced that we are called to use our gifts. Their pastor Gordon Cosby says, "If our potential is blocked and has found no creative channels in which to flow, then what we feel in the presence of another is envy—only a perplexing pain or deadness. We will have no praise of another—no joy in another. Instead, we will turn away and in subtle ways seek to destroy another. This is why we cannot get on with the business of loving unless we are discovering our own gift." This sounds like the perfect remedy for a boring, unsatisfactory retirement.

SIMPLICITY MADE SIMPLE

FIND VOCATIONAL GUIDANCE. Retirement is a time for realizing our full potential. Vocational guidance is not just for youth. It's important at all ages. And fortunately, many churches have realized this and are doing something about it. My church has a ministry that uses a Christ-centered approach to assist individuals who are unemployed, underemployed, or misemployed. Using a variety of resources, career explorers are given the opportunity to learn about their gifts, abilities and interests. Ultimately the outcome is for the career explorer to hear and follow God's calling in their careers now and in the future.

FIND YOUR GIFT. The process of searching for individual gifts is as important at seventy as it is at seventeen. Anna B. Mow, author of *So Who's Afraid of Birthdays*, says, "Don't be surprised at anything. Who knows? You might be a Grandma Moses." She began painting at seventy-nine. Seek your individual gifts under the guidance of the Holy Spirit. Don't be surprised if you are called to do something that you think you cannot. Remember that the Lord will never call you to a job that is "your size." He wants to challenge your faith by giving you "God-size" work.

SEEK AND YOU WILL FIND INCOMPARABLE BENEFITS from your work as a volunteer. Pat Watson, in her article "Volunteering after Retirement" for *Mature Living* magazine, said to follow the "Be" factors for a volunteer. *Be selective* by choosing areas of volunteerism in which you have a special interest or can make the greatest impact. *Be committed* by considering this a real job, as a contract between you and the person you work for. *Be sensitive.* Regardless of the area of work, volunteers will encounter people who need a listening ear, a tender touch or a word of encouragement. *Be flexible* by having an alternate plan available if unforeseen circumstances arise, especially with a program designed to entertain or instruct. *Be discerning* by honoring others with confidentiality. Relationships are built on trust. Above all, treat confidence with respect. And *be excellent*. The recipients of your volunteer work deserve the best you can offer.

**Lord, I believe there is something left for me to do.
Lead me through Your Word and circumstances
to show me how to contribute to the spiritual growth
of others. I am grateful for any opportunity to tell others
what I know to be true about You. Amen.**

What's Your Role in the Church?

They took palm branches and went out
to meet him, shouting, "Hosanna! Blessed is he
who comes in the name of the Lord! . . ."

—JOHN 12:13 (NIV)

Palm trees are known for their long lives. To flourish like a palm tree means to stand tall and to live long. Palms take three decades to mature but may live for two hundred years. Palms provided the branches that joyful crowds waved to welcome Jesus to Jerusalem. The Psalmist used palms as a symbol to remind us that honoring God is not limited to young people who seem to have boundless strength and energy (Psalm 92:12, 14). Even in old age, devoted believers can wave their palms to encourage others while still producing sweet fruit themselves. In fact, some might suggest that if our spiritual age is equal to our physical age, then we should be able to produce more spiritual fruit than when we were younger.

To survive spiritually, we must be connected in fellowship. This is true for churches as well. "And since we are all one body in Christ, we belong to each other, and each of us needs all the others" (Romans 12:5, NLT). The church needs *every* member of the body. Tony Evans says, "The church as the body of Christ grows when each and every individual part is doing its job and contributing to the whole. The growth of the church is nothing more than the growth of its members, since the church is a living organism made up of living parts." And the elderly are an essential part of that body.

Retirees should rank high among God's gifts to the church. God expects faithfulness from His children in all seasons of life. Churches, for their part, must provide opportunities for retirees to share their gifts. I read an article from the Canadian Conference of Mennonite Brethren Churches titled "Finding Fulfillment in Retirement" that said, "Older persons in the church are privileged people. They have accumulated many years of knowledge and experience. If retirement is viewed as an opportunity for growth and service, then faith will be strengthened and lives enriched. If, however, these years are seen only as a time for self-indulgence, followed ultimately by difficulty and degeneration, then they will be unproductive and disappointing indeed." In other words, these later years will no longer produce fruit. Our churches too will suffer without fruit-producing elders.

YOUR CHURCH STILL NEEDS YOU

Besides, where is it written that we should retire from church? A good retirement should include an ongoing involvement and relationship with your local church. Jack Stotts, a member of the Board of Pensions of the Presbyterian Church, says, "Retirement as a context, not a condition, reminds us that we will not be defined by our age or our setting in life. Our call is to respond to the ultimate calling of God, but now in a different context. There will not be, nor should there be, the expectation that we will be altogether different people with altogether different calls. What there will be is a change of priority or emphasis with some characteristics that endure."

Stotts also says that what we have to do is to discern those calls and accord them different measures of importance and significance while we retain the calling as what is central for our own integrity. As we put down one call, we pick up another or others. Stotts cites Joseph Haroutunian, professor of theology at McCormick Seminary in Chicago, who says we find ourselves having to grow into a new culture that is suitable for our new age. There is freedom in this new age. We are free from certain constraints and restraints. We are free to apply our gifts and talents in new situations. Stotts says, "In retirement we are free to venture into practices untried and even avoided, unable to claim 'too busy.' "

Most retirees and older people want to be useful. We don't want to suddenly end our involvement in our church. We want to serve. But churches must be willing to plan how to utilize this reservoir of time, talent and training. They must learn not to send signals, subtly or otherwise, that they expect retirees to retire from their kingdom service. There is no biblical basis for setting aside our work within the church to pursue only a life of secular leisure. Guideposts writer Carol Knapp has found the perfect role models in her mother and her friends for her own later years:

> My mother and her friends are the kind of people who keep this world spinning. They need glasses, those who aren't showing a little snow on the rooftop are using some camouflage, and

a couple of them are shorter than they used to be. Yet, in their seventies, they're filled with faith and excited about life.

Francis, for example, emigrated to the United States from Switzerland. She learned to speak English, but never learned to drive. When her husband of nearly fifty years died, she braved the Division of Motor Vehicles office, and after several attempts emerged with a new license. Never mind her twenty-mile distance restriction; she gets where she wants to go in her small, north Idaho town.

Helen is the romantic of the bunch. Though nearing eighty, she sits with stars in her eyes while she watches her favorite love story, *Random Harvest*, for the hundredth time.

Dolly is my mom's golf partner. They are first on the course several mornings a week, after Mom has indulged in her daily thirty-minute walk. Now Dolly is patiently learning to deal with her daughter's multiple sclerosis.

Dorothy, a retired college professor, once came "too close" to getting married. Instead, she keeps in close touch with her former students and always has fix-it projects going at home. She and Mom engage in lively debates from opposite sides of the political fence.

Their friends have taken their knocks in life. Yet every Sunday morning they are in church singing praises to God. And the rest of the week they are out enjoying His creation and serving others in His name. They are, to me, models of those "whose trust is the Lord" and my ideal of the woman I hope to become when I "get old."

SIMPLICITY MADE SIMPLE

REACH OUT TO ALL AGES. Sixteen-year-old Brandon Dauphinais wrote an amazingly insightful article in 2002 titled "The Age-Integrated Church," in which he said, "One should recognize that the leaders of the church go beyond just the ordained ministers; but parents, adults, senior adults, young adults and even older children are leaders in the church because all of these have someone looking up to them as a model. In this light, the modern age-segregated church conflicts with the training of leaders by isolating and splitting apart the separate ministries." Eric Wallace, in his book *Uniting Church and Home*, says, "Thus, the church's identity as a unified force—a set of interconnected relationships—is lost in the shuffle. By allowing our church to be exclusively need-driven or divided into groups by age and sex, we fail to equip people for the spiritual leadership of others.

BUILD HEART-LEVEL RELATIONSHIPS within an age-integrated ministry. Wallace says, "An integrated ministry uses heart-level relationships as its primary method for ministry because they are most effective. When heart-level relationships are the primary source of ministry, accountability is increased because deeper commitments mean more accountability among the members of the church." He also says that older men working with younger men and older women working with younger women is the prescription for relationship within the church. An age-integrated approach increases overall spiritual maturity in its members. It fosters people to reach out to each other beyond Sunday morning.

Appreciate wisdom. A Vatican document from October 1998 entitled "The Dignity and Mission of Aged Persons in the Church and in the World" called for new pastoral initiatives to address the needs of elderly people. It called for a renewed appreciation of the wisdom that has traditionally been recognized in older people, and encourages the elderly to recognize their own ability to bear witness to the truths of the Christian faith—including the witness of patient endurance for those who suffer from pain, neglect or infirmity. As the population ages, so too will the majority of churchgoers age. Unless we all **COME TO A NEW APPRECIATION FOR WHAT "ELDERS" CAN BRING** to the table, we will find ourselves spiritually starving to death. The church and the elderly themselves must realize that the future shape of the church is dependent on significant contributions and support from the elderly community. Churches must also recognize and provide special activities for their seniors by easily accommodating wheelchairs and walkers, and accommodating eyesight, hearing and other continence impairments. They can also remove emotional barriers that can result in alienation by encouraging the building of bonds between the elderly and other people in the congregation.

As I age, Lord, remind me not to be selfish with my time.
And while there are others who are still older than I,
remind me to ask them for the stories of Your faithfulness
in their lives so that I, too, will continue to grow
in the knowledge of Your power. Amen.

Defining Your Legacy

A good man leaves an inheritance
to his children's children. . . .

—PROVERBS 13:22 (NAS)

Ross Campbell and Gary Chapman, authors of the *Five Love Languages of Children*, wrote an article for Christian.com titled "We Should Leave Our Kids . . . More than Money" in which they say, "A legacy is an inheritance handed down from one generation to the next, something by which our descendants remember us. All the legacies we leave our children will affect their personal character. Three *nonmaterial* legacies, which will greatly influence the lives of those who follow us, are *moral*, *spiritual*, and *emotional*."

A *moral* legacy is our standard of beliefs of what is right and what is wrong. A *spiritual* legacy is what we believe about the nonmaterial world. What we leave our children depends on how closely our behavior correlates with our expressed beliefs. Campbell and Chapman say, "The heart of your legacy to your children is spiritual. Praying for your children daily is a living legacy that can influence their behavior now and for years to come." An *emotional* legacy depends on how we meet the emotional needs of children. Campbell and Chapman also say, "If their needs are met, they receive love, wholeness and balance—a positive emotional legacy. But, if they are not met, the children receive insecurity, low self-esteem and often fear—a negative emotional legacy."

According to The Legacy Project and their Legacies Across Generations effort, "Legacies are about life and living. They are about learning from the past, living in the present, and hoping for the future." In defining a legacy, The Legacy Project wrote this: "Where do you think it's best to plant a young tree: a clearing in an old-growth forest or an open field? Ecologists tell us that a young tree grows better when it's planted in an area with older trees. The reason, it seems, is that the roots of the young tree are able to follow the pathways created by former trees and implant themselves more deeply. Over time, the roots of many trees actually graft themselves to one another, creating an intricate, interdependent foundation hidden under the ground. In this way, strong trees share resources with weaker ones so that the whole forest becomes healthier."

YOUR LEGACY IS BEING FORMED

We thrive when we grow in the presence of those who have come before. Research shows that children develop better emotionally if they have four to six caring adults involved in their lives. Research also reveals that adults lose meaning in their lives if they do not have the sense that they are able to help those who come after them.

Grandparents are in a unique position to leave a meaningful legacy to their grandchildren. Psychoanalyst Erik Erikson, in his studies of the entire life cycle, coined the word "generativity" to identify the second to last stage of the eight stages into which he divided the human life cycle. The Legacy Project Web site summarizes Erikson's concept: "At its simplest level, generativity is about providing for succeeding generations. It's choosing to take an active interest in guiding the next generation. In its broadest sense, generativity is the desire to put your energy into things that will outlive you. It's a sense that your life is worthwhile and extends beyond yourself." It is a choice grandparents, grandfriends and others at this stage of life can make to be active in leaving a worthwhile legacy for those that follow.

As entrepreneur and author Paul J. Meyer says in his book *Unlocking Your Legacy*, "When all is said and done, each of us will leave only four things behind: Memories—thoughts that others have of us. Souvenirs—proof of our existence. Trophies—records of our achievements. Legacies—everything you are and possess today." Let's hope we can all leave as good a legacy as Guideposts writer Mary Lou Carney's mother did:

> I sit in the car, staring at Mother's house, waiting for the rest of the family to arrive. My sister Libby. Her daughter Carol. My own daughter Amy Jo. The numbness is starting to wear off now, and I feel grief gripping my heart like a vise. Mother is dead. I look at the house and think about how much she loved this small bit of real estate. Home. She'd always said she wanted to go straight from here to heaven, and she almost had. Just a few days in the hospital after the stroke.
>
> I gather my strength for the task at hand: cleaning out the house and going through Mother's stuff. I look at the cement goose on the porch, its purple bonnet askew and, through

tears, I smile. Purple. How Mother loved that color! From the carpet on the floor to the kitchen cabinets, she had surrounded herself with shades of lavender. I sigh, thinking of the crowded knickknack shelves, the stacks of periodicals, the cupboards and cabinets stuffed with a lifetime of stuff.

But even as I wave to my sister and step out of the car, I know our legacy is not here. Not in the paltry possessions Mother left behind. We've already seen our inheritance: in the hundred people who braved last night's weather to pay their respects at the funeral home; in the eulogy of the young man who sang at the funeral, talking about how Mother had been his favorite Sunday school teacher; in the dozens of flower arrangements that now covered her grave. One card read, "To Nancy, who introduced me to Christ."

This was what Mother left us. The things we have to sort and the decisions we have to make in the next few days are just details. The truly important stuff already has been taken care of.

SIMPLICITY MADE SIMPLE

CHOOSE TO LEAVE A RIGHTEOUS LEGACY. We certainly do not want to pass anything on to our children or grandchildren that would spiritually harm them. We do not want to leave them a legacy of apathy, anger, spiritual weakness, selfishness or worldliness. That means we must first be aware of the negative characteristics we may have received and make a conscious choice not to continue to pass them down to future generations. We must remember that we were redeemed. It takes a conscious decision and a deliberate effort to build a new life and a new legacy.

LEAVE A LEGACY OF LOVE. A legacy of love says that we love God with all our heart, mind, soul and strength (Mark 12:29–30). It says that God comes first, we love truth, we love our neighbors as ourselves and that we love our enemies as well as those near and dear to us.

Don't let distances keep you from leaving a legacy of beautiful memories for your grandchildren. An enterprising grandmother here in Lancaster County, Pennsylvania, started a new business, Nani's Sunshine Corner, which records grandparents reading stories to their grandchildren. The video is then mailed to the children who can now sit in front of their television set, press the remote control, and watch one of their grandparents appear on screen. If the child wants to "spend time" with his grandma, he can play the disc that has grandma reading. Technology is just one way to close the gap between families. But there are other **CREATIVE WAYS TO DO LONG-DISTANCE GRANDPARENTING**, such as creating a family newsletter as Louise Black has done. For the past ten years, she has published the family magazine, *Black on White* (the title plays on the family name of Black and the print on white paper stock). The bound publication includes family photos, letters, school essays, graphics and archival material—items of interest to her children's families alone. She said, "The grandchildren are thrilled to see their work published and they argue over who will get first chance at reading a new edition." Another creative granny has made six storybooks with family pictures. For each book, she made up a children's story. She puts the storybook together and then takes it to a photocopy store to be transferred to special, decorated children's paper, and then she laminates it and puts it into a spiral binder to send to all her grandkids.

GO CAMPING in style! Grand Camps combine an opportunity for heritage building with sun and fun. LifeQuest Ministries holds a summer camp program designed to help you bond with your grandchildren (ages seven to twelve) in a God-honoring way. According to Cavin Harper, president of LifeQuest, Grand Camps offer the opportunity to spend quality time with your grandkids while passing the torch of your spiritual legacy. Harper says, "Grandparents are in a unique position to connect with their grandkids at a soul level and help them understand such things as loving, giving, honesty, community, commitment, respect and honor, to name a few. Grand Camps are intended to challenge grandparents to rise up with renewed vision and vigor to assume this vital, God-ordained role." You can contact them at (866) 522-1404 or e-mail them at lifequest@grbonline.com.

Father, when my family reviews the history of my life story, I pray that Your forgiveness will blot out the pages that need to be forgotten and that Your grace will reveal the memories of Your blessings on our family. Your Word says in Exodus 20:5–6 that You will show love to a thousand generations that follow me—I give You thanks for a wonderful life. Amen.

Conclusion

Whether you are already retired or simply planning for your later years, I hope that I have helped to erase at least some of the "old" ways of thinking about later life and have helped you adopt a new and inspiring perspective. I hope too that you have sought God's point of view for your retirement years. He has plans for us—no matter how old we get. Aging is not for sissies. But we are blessed with a never-ending and abundant resource for living a life of purpose and growth with optimism and joyful hope.

Our hope is Christ. Our optimism is a choice we make in how we view this stage of life. We can grumble about our aches and pains. We can be content to simply relax and take it easy. Or we can choose to keep growing and offer our lives as a living sacrifice to God by embarking on a spiritual journey for the rest of our lives.

The baby boomer generation has always wanted to make a difference. Now, in retirement, we have the opportunity to prove our worth. But to be effective we must be careful to avoid disaster by planning well for our financial, physical and spiritual assets. If we act as good stewards, we can make a difference and accomplish the will of our Father. Our call has always been to respond to the ultimate calling of God, but now in retirement it takes on a different context. As our responsibilities are reprioritized it allows us to focus on things that we simply didn't have time for before retirement.

Consider this your time of true blessing. Just as Moses was able to tackle his greatest accomplishments with God's grace and strength in his later years so, too, can you.

Notes

Part One—Passionate about Retirement

1. Nancy K. Schlossberg, EdD, *Retire Smart, Retire Happy—Finding Your True Path in Life* (Washington, DC: APA Life Tools, American Psychological Association, 1979), 21, 38, 39.
2. Jane K. Belsky, PhD, *Here Tomorrow: Making the Most of Life After Fifty* (New York: Ballantine Books, 1988), 71.
3. Belsky, 83.
4. Phil Rich, EdD, MSW, Dorothy Madway Sampson, MSS, LCSW, and Dale S. Fetherling, *The Healing Journey Through Retirement: Your Journal of Transition and Transformation* (New York: John Wiley & Sons Inc, 2000), 156, 157.
5. Belsky, 92–93.
6. Mike Yorkey, *Your Fabulous Fifties: Answers to Your Most Asked Questions about Life After Fifty* (Colorado Springs: Victor Books, 2000), 42, 43.
7. Jeanette Lockerbie, *Fifty Plus* (Old Tappan, New Jersey: Fleming H. Revell, 1976), 53, 54.

Part Two—Simply Settled in Your Home

8. Hugh Downs, *Fifty to Forever* (Nashville, Tennessee: Thomas Nelson, 1994), 132, 138.

Part Three—Simply Smart Regarding Money

9. "What Money Type are You?" *Money* magazine (August 2005), 90.
10. Jan Cullinane and Cathy Fitzgerald, *The New Retirement* (Emmaus, Pennsylvania: Rodale, 2004), 412–415.
11. Ibid., 383.

Part Four—Simply Prepared for a Happy Life

12. "Brain-Healthy Lifestyle Is Best Defense Against Everyday Memory Problems," www.aarp.org.
13. Schlossberg, 138.
14. Ibid, 139.
15. "Look Who's Not Talking," *The Wall Street Journal Sunday* (September 4, 2005), 2.

Part Five—Simply Satisfied

16. Elizabeth O'Connor, *Journey Inward, Journey Outward* (New York: HarperCollins, 1968), 109.